STARCK
in
words

ISBN: 2-84426-209-0
N° Éditeur: 1207
Dépôt légal: March 2003

STARCK

in

words

Centre Pompidou

Valérie Guillaume

Foreword

This collection of writings on Philippe Starck runs in counterpoint to a brilliant exhibition that has been conceived as a work in and of itself. There, we discover a single actor with his "shadow" and some phantoms, a unique decor of eleven herms topped by video screens, and lastly, a "missal" to the exhibition serving as a user's guide. This enigmatic puzzle incarnates an unprecedented exhibition experience that dislocates the traditional grid of the viewer's path and de-structures the referential classification of works.

On the basis of a sentient "magma" of this sort, how does one go about constructing what could constitute a collection of analyses and interpretations? This book is organized in eight short essays that closely follow a few specific aspects in Starck's work, whether it concerns their philosophical (Michel Onfray) and semiotic (Benoît Heilbrunn) formulation or their return to the diverse fields of architecture (Sophie Trelcat) and design (Stéphane Laurent and Valérie Guillaume). In addition, three essays (Christine Colin, Vanni Pasca and Christopher Mount) enter the territories of European and American production and are rooted in inquiries about design's identity and recognition, which are constantly required to reconfigure themselves.

Whatever angle one takes to approach Philippe Starck, we grasp, through his very diversity, the constants that found his practice: his inspired and lucid sense of poetry, his omnipresent humor and his irrepressible freedom of speech.

Contents

Michel Onfray

The Anatomy of a Few Spells

Like in Maurice Ravel's only opera, *L'Enfant et les sortilèges* (The Child and the Magic Spells), Starck's objects talk, fly, crawl, swim, slide, sway, murmur in the silence and act; they generate magic, cast spells, spawn strange fascinations; they stir up deeds and misdeeds, changes in atmosphere, comfort and discomfort; they welcome or keep at bay; they constantly question and probe; they force, oblige and constrain. In a word, they do not leave indifferent a consciousness informed of their existence by the gaze, even if vague or furtive. Philippe Starck possesses a vocabulary, grammar and style—despite his disgust over the word—capable of defining a character and a temperament. I see in his work traces of a kind of shamanic alphabet that allows objects, not to have a soul, but to speak a language capable of relating the intimate life of things and hearing unheard-of words. Where a shaman would communicate with polar bears and arctic poppies, the bohemian artist converses with tables and houses, kettles and lighters, talks to chairs and sinks, and then has a serious discussion with door knobs. I propose twelve ways which may help pry open the mystery of this absurd affair's pathos.

ONE: A VOLUNTARIST AESTHETIC

First, let us consider the expansiveness and the number of fields taken up by this personality, then let us conclude that the artist's work has *a totalizing aesthetic* in the Hegelian sense: Philippe Starck includes, totalizes and embraces every object in the world and nothing less. From the smallest to the biggest, from the most innocent to the most symbolic, from crudest to the noblest, from the most impoverished to the most sophisticated, from the most ordinary to the most exceptional, not a single piece of concrete reality escapes him: from a poker to a building, from a lighter to an Olympic flame, from a toothbrush to a library, from a coat hook to a restaurant, from a noodle to a house. Not to mention glasses and motorcycles, radios and televisions, bathrooms, hotels and other extravagant objects . . .

From getting out of bed to going to bed, from waking up to falling asleep, the details of everyday life, the daytime ritual and the pagan liturgy all gain from it: getting up, washing up, getting dressed, lighting our surroundings, eating, moving about, finding a place to live, communicating, having fun, resting, relaxing. Everything comes in several versions and is inscribed in Philippe Starck's language. What is missing are a coffin, a cenotaph and objects of death—chandelier, censer and aspergillum to cover all possible fields—but the absence of thanatological references makes sense, since everything the artist touches is (used) for life and nothing else. Eros the libertine, Dionysus the raving mad, Proteus the multiple, Vulcan the blacksmith, Pygmalion the originator, yes; but not Thanatos the livid . . .

Designer obviously, architect of course, conceiver of forms and objects definitely, draftsman certainly, and a good many other activities fit if we really want labels. But these splintered worlds display a universality, a totality clearly designating the artist, one who emanates demiurge and powerfully transforms everything he touches. Woe to whatever his hands grab hold of, cursed be any material touched by his fingers, calamity for all matter that he nimbly palms, for the days of this metaphorical clay are therefore numbered and it is swiftly on its way to becoming a form, a force, a distinctive energy. In the beginning a sheet of paper, an iron rod, at the other end a lamp; at the starting point a textile, three bent tubes, upon arrival a chair; before a little flour, water and butter, after a pastry streamlined like a luxury Italian car. In between, a type of devilish genius with a Faustian laugh . . .

With Starck, objects resolve on their own, immediately and violently, the age-old antinomy between the ordinary item and the work of art. They bring an end to the mutilated world in which the crudeness of everyday life faces the exceptionalness of aesthetic production; they surpass the opposition between the material detail of the impure world and the abstract invisibility of the pure artistic sphere; they abolish the contradiction between the street and the museum, one's private home and the public collection. Art is no longer used to hoard, speculate on and gather in values in the hope that they will rise in value; it no longer has the function of acting as a social marker of a class lacking legitimatization and identity or tribal recognition; it is part of the real, it transfigures and erases the separations between the museum-related and daily life. Through it and with it, we can live in a museum in the comfort of our own homes.

TWO: IMMANENT METAPHYSICS

In addition to this radical revolution that makes it possible to not set aside art for art but to conceive it for life, for all moments of life, Philippe Starck also sets off *immanent metaphysics.* In other words, he commits an unpardonable sin in the contemporary art world, which is predominantly marked by Platonic transcendence of the idea, the concept, the unspeakable, the ineffable, and placed under the authoritarian auspices of a vaguely Debordian and truly trendy vulgate of fetishizing merchandise, spectacularizing the world and sacralizing the image.

Starck inverses the classical and conservative values of aesthetic postmodernity by asserting the excellence of a certain number of truly subversive values: immanence, matter, reality, object, the visible, the showable, incarnation and, worse yet, merchandise, spectacle and image. Unpardonable faults in this small, clerical world of today's nihilist, emaciated, empty and pallid artists. Each of his works insolently presents itself both as use value and exchange value, theater and circus, comedy and drama. Mixed genres, disreputable type . . .

Behind deceptive appearances, and in the purest Hegelian tradition of cunning reason, Starck rematerializes art. He hollows out, digs, smoothes, but under no circumstances does he strive for an improbable quintessence. When so many artists succumb to the allures of nihilism, to a gratuitous fascination for openings, holes, nothingness and emptiness, while in fact the echoes of minimal art and conceptual art—so old already—persist, weakened and exhausted; Starck drains to fill, he empties to saturate, he targets surface to create depth. He wills an effective form magnifying a pure presence in space and then creates the conditions of a pagan epiphany of matter; he thus creates material jubilation, and therefore a jubilant materialism.

THREE: A LITURGY OF THE OBJECT

These apparitions take place in the visible flesh of volumes that concentrate the artist's immanent metaphysics. Hence *a liturgy of the object*. These real fictions, these manifest virtualities constructed to compensate for the invisibility of forces and energies, belt along like atoms, monads, particles, asteroids, meteors or shooting stars. They move with the crawling or swaying of animals restive to fitting into a Linnaean nomenclature, they make bachelor machines of themselves or act like extravagant, extraordinary productions. Starck's objects populate a world, over which he sat enthroned as an efficient and humorous demiurge, before becoming its pagan priest brimming with vitality—he's no fool.

These objects reveal the presence of alternative worlds in the very tissue of reality. In a context without gods of an exhausted modernity that abhors life, health, joy, excess and serenity, this merry liturgy of the object builds an immanent religion; it opens onto a horizontal communion. The rematerialization of aesthetic contributes to the rematerialization of the world through a celebration of its slightest details. Like a fractal, what is possible in the very fiber of a thing, in its epicenter or its fringes, can be repeated throughout the entire universe. A form that comes from the artist's mind contaminates everything it meets.

To separate these objects from the world, in order to give them autonomy, a possibility of escaping heaviness, Starck tackles the laws of elementary physics.

Acting as a demiurge once again, he invents a flying lamp with no stand, strangely suspended in midair by a helium pocket; he constructs a panel that diffuses light at the source with no visible power supply, fed solely by a transmission of microwaves; he makes a bookcase with no apparent base, barely resting on a point that siphons off the forces of gravity to the floor. Each time a war breaks out against the spirit of heaviness, it targets the long-standing enemy: the laws of gravity, movement toward the ground—metaphors for the Fall of Man.

FOUR: A MINIMAL VOLUNTARISM

In this angel's fight against the ponderous demon, the artist displays *a minimal voluntarism*. This does not mean that his will is minimal, rather, it targets the minimal. Purging, rarefaction, reduction, extracting the essential: these are the objectives that go beyond baroque, rococo, mannerist or romantic aesthetics. This is the advent of a direct, efficient, bare, stiff, pure art. Lit on an operating table, burned to the bone in order to dig toward the marrow, Starck's scheme demonstrates that an essence and an existence, the idea and the perceptible, the noumenon and the phenomenal, cannot exist separately. In his view, and according to his works, the quintessential resides in the epicenter of matter, which, paradoxically, does not exclude setting up this center in the fringes, on the surface, on the skin of things. In the aesthetics of decentering, divine (and Pascalean!) art, the center is everywhere and the circumference is nowhere: the object wears its soul like a piece of clothing, like ontological thrift shop clothes.

Bringing form out of matter—old scholastic passions!—allows the essence to emerge. Every object that Starck touches obeys this law and highlights a form that teams up with a locatable, clearly recognizable force. Even in the work of those who copy him . . . The unfailing proof of style is the existence of epigones. And the world that the artist created is not lacking in imitators or parasites. Essence revealed by a will indiscriminately presents itself to the gaze of anyone. It swathes, covers and coats, it sucks up from the center a power that spreads over the surface, it will go to the core to get what is needed for irrigating the skin, it plunges toward the soul and brings identity back to the surface.

FIVE: A VITALIST TROPISM

This talent for bringing light back up from the core to the fringes also reveals *a vitalist tropism*. At every opportunity, Starck shows a passion for organic forms and forces, which he stages in multiple variations. In most of the objects he invents, we find obvious morphological quotations from nature, in this instance from physiology, anatomy, zoology or osteology. On the shelves of my bookcases, I have the vertebras of a seal, a polar bear, as well as a man and a Mediterranean cetacean. They could stand comparison with Starck's armchairs, seats or other pieces of furniture.

Wings, holes, curves, distribution of forces, concretions, volumes, anchor points, symmetries, dynamics, everything works as a counterpoint: the creator of man, nature in this case . . . and the creator of objects draw from the same sources: life. Both confess a fascination for the answers offered to the problems posed by a tension, a passage, a flux or an energy. At the points where a nerve or vessel goes through or where a muscle is attached appear orifices, which in the artist's work provide balance, lift, stability, elegance and presence.

The correspondence between natural forms and cultural creations is also justified when a certain number of singular objects (claws, teeth, horns, as well as shells or fishbones, cartilage, or else a ray, a shark fin, a butterfly wing or even a mouse's tail) are put side by side with Starck's works. Against the tyranny of straight lines, horizontals, verticals, against the empire of abscissas and ordinates, of geometry and mathematics, he (re)deems the seductive sinuosity of biology and bionics, the flexible line, the curved volume, the playful boss, the voluptuous line, the jovial form, the extravagant diagonal, the mysterious folding and the unexpected arrangement. Life versus death, the invasion of plants and animals versus mineral rarity. The voluptuous Eros triumphs yet again . . .

SIX: A PLAYFUL MISE EN SCÈNE

Eros and a laughing god. Obviously, in the heavens inhabited by divinities, all divinities, in the ether saturated by the jealous God of monotheists, there is no laughing . . . It is difficult to imagine Jehovah, Mohammed or God doubled up laughing, or even simply smiling, or just making a vague gesture toward a similar expression . . . Seriousness reigns absolutely in the heavenly kingdom. In his work, Starck accentuates *a playful mise en scène*, which, let us agree, annoys the sad knights of contemporary art, and even the philosophers, intellectuals and other writers who are also convinced that if one wants to prompt laughter or smiles, it is impossible to be serious. To cut oneself off from this small world, there is nothing like a simple bet on irony, humor or amusement. Starck's world provides abundant occasions to do so.

Hence, there is more reference to the world of comic books than to the Sistine Chapel, and he quotes people like Glenn Baxter, for example, more frequently than Michelangelo. Speech bubbles and comic strips more than church ceilings or paintings on canvas, heroes dressed like Tintin more than demigods escaped from a Velásquez . . . A sin against good taste and all the references that classify, distinguish and aggregate one into a particular world. Quoting a comic book inevitably makes enemies among the pompous who saturate their obscure discourses with profuse approximate citations of postmodern philosophers. Nietzschean laughter destroys everything that nihilism produces, that trains conservative reflexes and that nurtures reactionary sluggishness. Laughing and prompting laughter, smiling and making others smile, that is a detestable pleasantry for those who manage the national business of intellectual matters.

Starck commits the same lapse of taste when he makes reference to science-fiction literature rather than the canonical authors "psalmodied" in the style of whirling dervishes by a large part of the socialite intelligentsia. Starck's pieces of furniture and objects, and even his houses come from illegal, outside, unexpected, unanticipated and untimely worlds: Alice in Wonderland's bedroom rather than the Verdurin salon. The artist evolves aesthetically on the other side of the looking glass rather than in the chic and conventional *arrondissements*. Each of Starck's creatures gives the impression that it will speak up and voice its opinion in a speech bubble . . .

SEVEN: A SOCRATIC INTERACTION

This frequent invitation to laugh is a product of *a Socratic interaction* that recruits objects in a joyful maieutic process. Things investigate, question, rouse and beckon the onlooker or user. They do not languish in silly, inane attendance or in passive and incredible stupidity. For they expect much from the humanoid looking them up and down. In using an armchair that one is afraid will tip over, in trying to rediscover the vanished function of a lamp masked, disguised and drowned in a form that hides its primary intention and purpose, in forcing one to solve the mystery of a metallic insect of the third kind concealing a lemon squeezer, the artist implicates and sweeps up the user in his adventure.

In the game proposed by Starck, objects are humanized and human beings are objectified, animals are mineralized and plant life is hominized: the face of a lamp is also an animal reference to the ray, the volume of a skull recalls the warrior's helmet of a Japanese building, the clawed legs of an insect refer to the prickly stem of a rose or to stylized limbs of an arachnidan mutant—the ranges merge, loot each other, quote each other, interpenetrate and impregnate each other, they feed off and then give birth to new morphologies. In these farcical collisions, the mechanical replicates the living. And we come across Bergson's definition of laughter again. Playful reality turns into ironic reality. Like Socrates, the objects probe human beings, question them and obtain smiles and amazement from them.

EIGHT: THE KINETICS OF METAMORPHOSES

Within these processes of transformation and transmutation, reality experiences different states. Hence torsions, anamorphoses, slides and changes in texture evoking computer-generated morphing. This *kinetics of metamorphoses* displaces boundaries and, in the etymological sense, it de-forms. It undoes forms in order to redo them, otherwise and elsewhere. Roles are continuously exchanged between inanimate objects and animate human beings, dead things and living animals, static matter and dynamic energy. Philippe Starck's reality consists merely of the continually changing sum of modifications of a single substance.

A horn or a tear is turned into a vase, a spermatozoid is transfigured into a poker, a claw becomes a closet door, a shark's tooth protrudes from the wall to serve as a coat hook, a series of molar teeth pop up from the floor to offer seating, mutilated spiders straddle their three legs over a glass and trickle sour lemon, a golden larva wriggles on the rooftop of a Japanese restaurant, jellyfish simulate a long translucent immobilization and metamorphose into stools, ribcages dried to the bone lean up against a wall to serve as bookcases: the world swarms, murmurs and heats up—dry, lukewarm or humid with potentialities in labor.

The interim is where the artist captures and freezes the metamorphosis: not anymore but not yet. Far from the starting point and not yet reaching the destination. The shift happens at an imprecise, invisible moment. Indeed, we can see what was there and of course we witness what it has become, but we wonder about the practical details of this passage. When did the magic take effect? The eye seems to be incapable of stopping the movement during the magic junction between the two instances. Starck seizes the moment of loss of balance between two equilibriums, then he transfigures this moment of instability into a new stability. Demiurgical devil . . . In the new object, signs from both worlds persist: the ray and the lamp copulate in a teratological manner to produce a monstrous object, a chimera, biologists would say. Starck is an inventor and a chimera breeder. This kinetics amounts to a method for producing the aforementioned unprecedented creatures.

NINE: THE PHYSICS OF BALANCE

By playing on the ambiguity of these two shores, the artist juggles with a singular *physics of balance*. Fascinated by what does not look like it will hold but in fact does hold, mischievous in its persistence to propose an apparent instability that marvelously conceals an astonishing stability, Philippe Starck makes us nervous, he excites the nerves and works up the nervous system: sitting down on an object that surely causes falls? Finding the appropriate physiological posture with that thing impossible to mount, grasp or ride? Washing one's hands using this installation with hidden or even inexistent mechanisms? Turning on a lamp lacking a switch? Lining up books on a shelving unit that barely touches the floor, and putting oneself right in the midst of an imminent collapse?

The troubling proposition disturbs, it makes one uncomfortable and seems to relate the object back to the area of decoration, of intellectual, conceptual or formal achievement. At no time do we imagine use as a possibility. Beautiful, but not practical, pleasant to look at, touch and consider, but only good for the eye, not the body . . . Error: the body is stable, seated, composed, comfortable, relaxed, nicely settled in—surprisingly, that is the result. Once again, there is a variation on the theme of playful mise en scène and the bizarre, of a disparity between the premise, the anticipated and the outcome. In any case, this is a wonderfully ironic lesson: appearances are misleading; reality always conceals itself; authenticity cannot be revealed until it has been tested by the world. Truth is embedded in the false.

TEN: THE AERONAUTICS OF FORCES

Stability demands a mastery of forces. Including a mastery of the artist's favorite element: air, space. Hence *the aeronautics of forces.* This not only makes reference to avionics or his father's profession, or even to his slightly daredevil exploits as a pilot, but also to the avowals of a favorite element among pre-Socratic philosophers. For, unquestionably, Philippe Starck is jubilant in, with, by and for air, including its liquid form: water. There is no terra firma for this man who spends his life contradicting the laws of gravity . . . Homage to Bachelard's clouds, sky, birds, flight, Icarus, winds, breeze and the Holy Ghost. Spirit. Consider helium, kites, pennants, flags, airplane wings and the inflatable houses of the artist's youth . . . Ethereal grammar.

Resorting to a helicopter manufacturer to obtain materials flirting with immateriality concretizes and manifests this constant yearning for more air and lightness. A strong lift, much resistance, and maximum densities—they all illustrate a metaphysics of forces: the least to say the most, the minimum in drawing to express a maximum, the rare for characterizing the precious, material in order to expound the immaterial. It is a playful and ironic search for points of rupture and loss of balance, recurrent desire for stability and balance, crystallized realizations of successful moments in these metamorphoses, taming and control of fierce violence turned into active forces: the silent object is always telling of the violent soul that inspired it.

An immanent reality, a purged voluntarism, a celebration of organic forms, a mise en scène of the bizarre, a passion for anamorphoses, a sublimation of steadiness, a dialectic of forms and forces—all this allows one to grasp the shamanism at work in Philippe Starck's objects. The speech of objects, communication of things, interactions between human beings and furniture, between living beings and materials, the glossolalia necessary for attaining rhythms, sung and murmured melodies: we hear a ceremonial, magic and mysterious music, we catch a fragment of the pagan mystic's chanting, a voice coming from nowhere, nourished by the spirit of animals, the soul of beasts and the breath of materials. Leather, paper, aluminum, wood, epoxy, glass and steel modulate their voices like ancestors skillful in shamanic ceremonies.

ELEVEN: A HEDONIST UTILITARIANISM

The whole of Philippe Starck's work culminates in an ethic that prefigures a type of politics. First, with a hedonist utilitarianism, then with an aristocratization of the consumer. First, *a hedonist utilitarianism*. Art separated from life generates an elitist aesthetic that begs, demands and necessitates initiation, the exchange of codes, the sharing of values handed down; art reconciled with life leads to a truly democratic aesthetic that uses the object to disturb and convert the subject. Far away from the museum, in one's home, the most mundane object is charged with an initiatory force and a value. Interceding not just for itself, it shows what goes beyond it but that is nonetheless embedded in it.

Useful and pleasant, practical and beautiful, functional and artistic—something that hangs out to dry one of the canons of Kantian aesthetics, which presupposes disinterested satisfaction. What pleases is useful too; what is useful can also please. With a dual effectiveness, the object satisfies one particular function and transmits what is beyond—elegant, agreeable,

seductive, indeed, but also beautiful and sometimes sublime. Such is the case for the toothbrush, which is mundane by definition since it comes under the intimate range of personal hygiene: Starck takes it out of the bathroom, without it necessarily making it lose its place or stop playing its role there. Delightful for both the dentist and the aesthete . . .
Beauty does not participate in an exterior essence of the object; beauty emanates from it. Ironically, it can even come from the places most contrary to the classical mediums of art: plastic—and not in bronze, gold or marble. It is abundant on the market, not rare and maintained as such for obvious lucrative reasons; cheap and not boosted by capitalist logic; immediately accessible intellectually and aesthetically by its seductive, direct and efficient form; triumphant in the most unexpected place for an art object, the toothbrush acts as a manifesto of this transformation from ordinary utility to real pleasure.

TWELVE: AN ARISTOCRATIZATION OF THE CONSUMER

The object's practice of distributing art in a miniscule, homeopathic, but daily manner results in an interesting *aristocratization of the consumer.* Every individual put in the presence of an object thought up, willed, created, produced and sold by Philippe Starck has his or her home transformed into a museum. By reversing the habitual movement that leads the art lover to exhibition rooms, Starck fulfilled a wish that was dear to poets who aspired to an active poetry that went out into the streets. This time, it enters the private individual's home, gets down from the pedestal where the elite, the bourgeois, the snobs and the conservatives keep it, and joins the smallest detail of daily life. When Duchamp called for the abolition of sterile artistic areas, he opened the way to dreamers who surprise with the bizarre, create strangeness, seek the unexpected and create poetry in the intimacy of the most banal existence, at the most unexpected moment, in the least appropriate place.

Defensible elitism presupposes the aristocratic proposition of an art offered to the greatest number of people; the indefensible version restrains its practice to a handful of elects on the principle of tribal co-optation. Philippe Starck sets in motion an education of the masses. To the greatest number of people, he distributes forms that educate the eye, prepare it, and train it to enter a domain where the arrangement of a larger quantity of forms can be envisaged in an increasingly complex manner. The morning brushing of one's teeth, provided that it is accompanied by an intelligent, playful, cheerful and educational relationship to the object, leads more surely to an understanding of the economy of an architectural structure—like one of Starck's magnificent buildings in Japan, for example—than would numerous didactic treatises on art. From the minute to the immense, Starck marks out the paths that reconcile aesthetics, ethics and politics. His art is the complete opposite of kitsch—reactivated lately by a few dreary big names in contemporary art—which is a product of demagoguery in that it gives people what they expect, without ever requiring any effort on their part, keeping them in mediocrity, flattering their taste for the flashy, the bulky and the crude; like his objects, his art draws the viewer up toward the top, producing an intellectual current of air. As far as art is concerned, kitsch cements demagogic religions; Starck's aesthetic, on the other hand, founds a democratic religion, a type of jubilant shamanism, an alternative to nihilism . . .

Translated by Elizabeth Jian-Xing Too

Benoît Heilbrunn

The Grandesigner

Brief Handbook of Starckian Philosophy

In memory of Louis Marin

"Really give of yourself.
Please don't send me
Another messenger.
They can't tell me what I want."[1]

"Any old object,
even the most ordinary,
contains ingeniousness,
choices and a culture."[2]

There is no disputing the fact that Philippe Starck has a place all of his own in the design world, both through the objects and the places he has thought up—and the way they disconcert us—and through the legitimizing approach with which he is forever accompanying his work as a designer. In order to grasp the principle and the challenges of his philosophy of the object, we shall try to highlight the major features of what we shall call a *mythical approach* to design. And we shall do this by taking a look both at Starck's different productions and at the various paratexts[3] which go hand-in-hand with them.

DESIGN... AND DESIGN... AND DRAWING

Contrary to what might be suggested by a naïve approach, the role of the designer (and a fortiori of Starck) is not confined to working out formal, chromatic and material codes for the object. It really consists, as is shown incidentally by the etymology of the word "design" [Lat. *designare*, to mark out, *disegno*...], in permanently associating a design with a drawing—in other words, a project and a form. To do this, the designer sets himself essentially at the crossroads of two dimensions: an *endomorphic* dimension that encompasses the formal and chromatic identity of membership, making it possible to assign the object to a given category of products; and an *exomorphic* dimension, encompassing an identity of differentiation whereby the object has peculiar features that set it apart from the other objects in its category and in some way make it legitimate on the market. The endomorphic dimension thus ensures that the object belongs to a given category of products (this is the axis of membership and similarity), whereas the exomorphic dimension emphasizes a factor of innovation and rupture with regard to market codes (this is the dimension of differentiation and otherness). So how are we to understand Starck's project?

The designer quite clearly favors the exomorphic dimension, and, by way of an attempt at ongoing re-semanticization on more and more competitive markets, his project ushers in a shift in relation to the codes in force. Starck actually denies having a purely decorative vision: "I'm all for economy," he says, "in the psychoanalytical sense of the term. Economical for everything. A product that achieves its obligation with a minimum of means. I like to touch things at the root, at the point where no more division is possible. The simpler an object is, the harder it is to make it: decoration always conceals something else."[4]

Despite this desire to get back to the essential and defining properties of the object, the Starckian object is nevertheless rooted in a permanent desire for de-banalization, and, even if it does significantly modify the world of signs traditionally associated with him, he does extract the product as much as he possibly can from its mere user value. This, incidentally, is what may lead to a denial of the object in its ordinarily accepted sense. Starck accordingly offers the following explanation, with regard to the toothbrush "designed" for Fluocaril: "I created that toothbrush because it's a basic non-product. Everybody needs one, and they're all much the same. But I thought that if in the morning you have something bright and cheerful on the shelf waiting for you, it would be like opening the bathroom window onto a summer landscape every day."[5] This game precisely helps to extricate the object from its user value "[lending requirements] a fifth dimension, a depth that gives a necessary object the opportunity to speak of other things."[6]

In spite of this claim of non-decorative design, Starck's project does refer to a formal innovativeness that tends toward a redefinition of objects and places, with as a corollary, for users, a shift in the values which they usually project onto them. In this accepted sense, "designing" an object is tantamount to redefining its functions and hence its defining components, whence—as we shall see in due course—the constant need to develop paratexts aimed at justifying it on an ongoing basis.[7]

It is actually possible to look at the object in two ways: as a utensil and a means, or, conversely, as an end, a "form of our being." This distinction between what is by agreement known in semiotics as a user program and a life program makes it possible to identify four ways of developing and promoting an object or place:

• A utilitarian development hallmarked by its signally concrete and utilitarian end purpose; the object is appreciated and sought out for its "practicality," its functionality, its comfort, its performance, its efficiency and the ease with which it may be used.

• A critical development that complements the utilitarian one, tallying with a logic of distancing, calculation and comparison; the object here is subject to assessment criteria inspired by external factors, and sought out for its value-for-money—qualitative and quantitative alike—its economy, its safety and its guarantees...

• An existential development which is seen as the exact contradiction of the previous approach; it corresponds to the "higher" expectations of people such as self-fulfillment and things to do with their aesthetic sense; the object becomes a conveyor to do with surpassing and realizing, of something that helps consumers to express their identity, their quest for adventure and their life projects.

• A larksome development, going hand-in-glove with the one above, which, essentially, has to do with emotions and sensations, or, alternatively, luxury; the object must, above all, be a source of feeling, pleasure, distraction, refinement...

Starck's program swiftly offers a glimpse of a paradox insomuch as his discourse is forever wavering between these four methods of development, braced in particular against a tension between the critical promotion and the utopian promotion of the object. So, to take up the example of the toothbrush, this is described turn by turn as being "made to remove scraps of meat from between the teeth"[8] (a markedly critical promotion) and "like opening the bathroom window onto a summer landscape every day" (an existential promotion). Similarly, Starck asserts that "a hotel is above all the quality of the pillow," but, in tandem, he says that visiting the Mondrian Hotel is nothing less than "living within a sunny cloud, together with the angels," and that the pool room in the Hudson Hotel is "a haunted castle where each door reveals an extraordinary scene."[9] In an ongoing way, his discourse sets up linkages between the grandiose and the tiny, the spectacular and the commonplace. As we shall see, the inner contradiction of the discourse based on the articulation of opposing ways of developing and promoting things actually represents the fundamental force that drives the Starckian dynamic.

THE CONTRADICTORY VIRTUES OF UTOPIA

As, if I may remind you, the economic virtue of Starckian design consists in amplifying the perceived value of the product in order to heighten its economic value, it can be said that what is involved is an interplay on the user value aimed at altering the exchange value and the sign value of the object. When the method of promotion chosen is essentially larksome or existential, the designer's work makes it possible to significantly increase the object's perceived value—otherwise put, its price. The goal earmarked for this type of design is undeniably the creation of an economic goodwill. The fact is that in a consumer culture where consumers are increasingly informed about marketing processes, it is hard to display this objective, whence the development of paratexts with a twofold function: they make it possible to legitimize the object by projecting it within a narrative (a narrative of origins, in particular) and likewise to articulate other methods of promotion, in particular ethical (see, for example, the importance of the "moral market" in Starck's work), which will act as an ultimate justification of the extra value of the economic object.[10] Whence the "tripod" which lies at the base of the object for Starck: aesthetic value, ethical value and economic value. This is how we can grasp the designer's creed: "Find, collect, correct and create, when necessary, honest, responsible, people-friendly objects. Objects that aren't necessarily beautiful, but sound objects."[11] The apparent denial of the aesthetic value, which is coherent within the context of an anti-decorative discourse, actually helps to legitimize the ethical value of the object and, thereby to create an economic goodwill.

In the Starckian project, the value of the object emerges from a constant tension between critical values and existential values, in other words, in semiotic terms, between a user program and a life program. This is why Starck displays not only a desire to work out "non-products" for "non-consumers"[12] (so as to de-alienate the consumer) but also, and at the same time, which may seem contradictory, a desire to design "honest, responsible, people-friendly objects [so that] a new relationship may occur between people, production and objects."[13] This paradoxical coexistence explains the permanent wavering in strategies devised to legitimize the Starckian object between user values and aesthetic values. There is a perfect illustration of this in the Richard III armchair "covered with warm brown leather, resembling from the front a club chair, but with the traditional back scooped out to reveal the steel frame," with regard to which Starck explains: "From the front, it's wholly bourgeois, but empty once you turn it round. I like that touch of hypocrisy."[14]

So it is absolutely possible to talk about a utopian project with Starck[15] insofar as utopia sets up an ideal imaginary mode which works in the mode of pure totalization, for it is not actually possible to conceive of any utopia "without this project of associating in a circumscribed place everything that man may think and experience in terms of ideals."[16] The utopian world is precisely the one whose ideal character perforce takes charge of some of the inner contradictions, precisely because, by way of an encompassing discourse which sorts out the said contradictions, utopia marks the triumph of the systematic mind. Whence the fact that the coherence within any utopian discourse is paradoxically conditioned by a necessary resolution of contradictory power games. The program works henceforth like a myth as defined by Claude Lévi-Strauss, namely as "a means of symbolically resolving antinomies, contradictions and unthinkable or unassumable conflicting situations, by including them within the layered structure of a narrative."[17] It now behooves us to understand what may in fact be covered by the notion of *mythical design*. Or, in other words: how are we to envisage the Starckian project, especially in the specific relations it is forever forming between the form and function of objects and places?

THE SWITCH-OVER OF FORM AND FUNCTION

With possible values invested in the object, it is now conceivable to associate a second level of analysis to do with its forms and its functions. It is actually possible to consider that, in an explicit or implicit way, design states a certain discourse about the "reality" of the object, in other words, it expresses its end purpose or, more accurately, the functions which are assigned to it from the outset. By admitting that design refers to a basic ancestral relationship between form and function—insomuch as it articulates a drawing and a design, to wit, a project and a form—then, depending on whether the design aims to "represent" or else to "construct" the function of the object, it is possible to envisage at least four ways of understanding the relationship between form and functions. A semiotic square[18] will help us to highlight the different creative approaches where design is concerned.

Typology of design philosophies

Significance of the endomorphic dimension	Significance of the exomorphic dimension
▼	▼
Referential design Representational system Form represents function Logic of conformity and compatibility Utilitarian promotion of the object E.g. Braun razor Marie robot (Moulinex)	**Mythical design** Constructional system Form (re-)creates function Logic of impact and rupture Existential promotion of the object E.g. Fluocaril toothbrush, Juicy Salif, Hot Bertaa (Starck)
Substantial design Non-constructional system Form incorporates function Logic of conformation Critical promotion of the object E.g La Marie (Starck), the Perrier glass (Szekely)	**Oblique design** Non-representational system Form exceeds function Logic of surprise Larksome promotion of the object E.g Mister Meumeu, Richard III, Louis XX, This is not a wheelbarrow (Starck), the kettle (Graves), the “King-Kong” family (Alessi), the iMac, etc.

In just a few words for each one, let us attempt to define these design philosophies, before actually getting to grips with the specific nature of the Starckian project.

REFERENTIAL DESIGN

Form may be closely compatible with the functions earmarked for the object. In such cases, the term referential design is used, insofar as the role of design is to produce a form whose main virtue is to display the object's function in a very exact way. Here we are in the realm of a very utilitarian approach to design, propped up by an indicial function limited to showing what the object might be used for. This, for example, is the whole meaning behind the functionalist project as well as a school like the Bauhaus, whose sacrosanct formula was "form follows function." A brand like Braun can be regarded as representative of this approach inasmuch as it has always advocated a "new culture of the (wished for) honest and human product, free of all deceptive ornamentation. The form of the appliance is determined just by its function..."[19]

SUBSTANTIAL DESIGN

Substantial design is based on an economy of meaning and means, and is thus aimed at taking the object at its root. Because form must take a back seat so as to highlight the substance of the object, we find here a clearly displayed refusal of ornamentation and grandiloquence. One of the undisputed representatives of this approach is Martin Szekely, well-known for his aversion to demiurgic artists. For example, he says with regard to the glass designed for Perrier: "An object designs itself [...]. It is its use—here, drinking—which determined this simple ancestral goblet shape." Design, here, almost refers to a desire to no longer design. He accordingly has this to say about glass dishes: "These dishes are reduced strictly to matter [...]. I want to construct with nothing. An object must merely separate man from the ground, enabling him to sit, eat... nothing more."[20]

Let us now deal with the other two approaches which seem alternately to hallmark Starck's work—to wit, oblique design and, to a greater degree, mythical design.

OBLIQUE DESIGN

By rejecting a purely referential approach, oblique design strives to look at the object in an indirect—oblique—and ironical way. Because the task of design is to signify that the object is not reduced to a set of functional aspects, form, here, cannot just be a carbon copy of the function earmarked for the object. It goes further. The sense of the object is not immediately forthcoming; it is a project to be constructed. So it is no more or less a matter of a play on objects or, alternatively, as Francis Ponge would put it, a eulogy of the "obgame." But what is the game if not, as it so happens, a discrepancy included within the framework of our shared representations, a shift of the eye around the object, a way of taking a fresh look at it with a new way of seeing, both in its form and its function(s). The game must here be understood in the sense of: "There's a game": the object—which was previously offered, like an item of evidence, in a sort of limpidity and routine and purring banality—once again presents a resistance to the eye and the hand, and is no longer rendered material in its usual texture. Playing with it thus means letting yourself be played with by it, letting yourself be taken by surprise, and surprised. Whereas it had become a sort of manipulated thing, with neither respect nor affect, it is once again an object, that is to say, a meaningful cultural artefact. The oblique side of Starck's design, in this new way of looking at the object, and re-investing it with new values, requires that conventions be broken. It just so happens that this approach makes it possible to reconstruct the reality of the object by coming up with a new interpretation of it, one which staggers it in relation to expectations in force, and informs a history or, more precisely, a narrative. So the designer tries to create a relationship of playful and ironical connivance with the user by means of the many paratexts aimed at explaining and legitimizing the object, as in the case of Mister Meumeu and the Richard III and Louis XX armchairs. This oblique design is altogether complementary with the mythical aspect of Starckian design, on which we shall now focus.

MYTHICAL DESIGN

The aim of mythical design, of which Philippe Starck is probably the most illustrious representative, is literally to re-create the object. It is important to make as clean a break as possible with codes and make this break quite obvious for users. So in this approach there is something of the demiurge, tending to think that the object must, over and above its user value, communicate feelings and emotions.[21] So the bachelor's pillow can "offer affection when you might need some at certain moments." Similarly, Starck talks about "the hotel business as therapeutic," insofar as "[his] hotels are inner journeys [...], itineraries of mental trips."[22] This is why the Starckian object is very often removed from any apparent end purpose, and becomes a poetic object in its own right, independently of any utilitarian or practical function. It thus becomes something other than what it was meant to be—from the consumerist viewpoint—it becomes worthy of interest for its own sake, free to be grasped as a pure object of aesthetic emotion, beyond any predetermined use. The Fluocaril toothbrush is undeniably more than a toothbrush and, as such, something other than a simple toothbrush. A distortion of meaning is added to the supplement of meaning. The co-existence of its harmonious lines and its stand gives a glimpse of an essentially playful and decorative intent, no longer an exclusively utilitarian one. This transfer of a utilitarian aim to an aesthetic one jointly implies a redefinition of the role of the object, without there being in any way whatsoever any question of doing away with its end purpose; it can actually be reckoned that what occurs is a re-switching of the end purpose of the object from a functional sector toward a more existential sector. What is involved here is simply the re-investment of an object—often regarded as commonplace—with emotional values. We find ourselves here faced with a veritable desire to cast a new spell on the object, or even lend it a euphoric quality again—and thereby do the same for the humdrum. Design thus turns into a harbinger of a better world.

Needless to say, Starck's program cannot suffer from any direct and transparent exposure; it ultimately comes across in a herald-like way, not unlike a God emerging masked. Over and above the incessantly reasserted importance of the hidden and the anonymous in his propositions ("Others are looking for form. I myself am looking for more anonymity"), a painstaking consultation of certain convergent appliances in the Good Goods catalogue will help us to show that Starck's program really does work in the manner of an Annunciation. But what is an Annunciation, if not the presentation of a dissemblance with regard to a horizon of expectations? Mythical design, as we have seen, is based on a reconfiguration of the consumer's expectations by way of an emphasis on the exomorphic dimension of the object. It is based on an operation of de-figuration/re-configuration, and operates on the model of dissemblance, in other words, difference, shift and detour. In other respects, Annunciation implies the updating of a general system of visibility (Annunciation refers precisely to what "is" but is not yet "appearing"), at work, for example, in the T-shirt for pregnant women, whose function is to reveal outside what is inside.[23] This system of visibility is, obviously enough, bound up with the idea of advent, as notably illustrated by the predominance of white and of the theme of the Nativity in the Good Goods catalogue. But the most worrying element is probably the presence of Mary, by way of a chair which, in Starck's own words, is "humility given to the object." The object becomes "something next to nothing," the "least possible"; it becomes the server of a message (and thereby an intercessor), and, from a religious angle, must "disappear so that there is no longer any trace of an order. It is limited to touches, looks and the voice" (like a reminder of the signs of the Annunciation). The presence of Mary very obviously calls to mind the presence of the Angel, who is none other than Dr. Skud, who, Starck tells us, is a "little guardian angel." Lastly, as in Renaissance paintings, each object is accompanied by a *festaiuolo*, a kind of witness character who warns readers and tells them about what is going on in the picture. The *festaiuolo* also plays a part of injunction to the Renaissance by warning onlookers not only about what is going on in the picture but also what should be going on in front of the picture. This is precisely the role of the paratexts which go with each object, and which have a role that is both descriptive and prescriptive.

THE GOD-DESIGNER OR: THE MEANING OF LIFE...

We have every cause to wonder whether the culminating point of this essentially mythical approach to design does not make some surreptitious reference to a sort of deification of the designer, with this latter playing a demiurgic role which can be read at varying levels: when he creates names (Pala Pala, Dr. Skud, Moosk, etc.), when he subjacently lets objects do the talking or, at least, when he gets them to live like subjects (the Starck eyes glasses, for example, manufactured on the model of the human body), or again when he devises animate or anthropomorphized objects.[24] This demiurgic power can also be read in Starck's self-asserted capacity to transfer powers to the consumer, as in the case of Starcknaked, which "might be that magic wand which gives women the freedom to choose who they want to be, where and when they want."[25]

Lastly, the demiurgic character of the Starckian approach is tried out essentially in the factitive character of objects, in other words in their capacity to get users to act in a certain way, by prompting gestural sequences and even affective schemes. The power of the demiurge is transformed into a governing power over bodies and souls, in the Foucauldian sense, where power is precisely what refers to the capacity to act (indirectly) on the way others behave. Governing here means structuring the possible field of action of others by, in particular, organizing the way in which individuals see the world. Most of Starck's objects are endowed with a very strong prescriptive power (they urge people to act, do and think in a certain way), which goes well beyond the commercial life, as is illustrated by the TeddyBearBand: "In favor of a single love, I dreamed of a single toy, a kind of training for a long-lasting attachment."[26] So it is easier to understand why the Starckian project is, fairly and squarely, a utopian project insofar as utopians are not merely world repairers; rather, they embody a demiurgic desire aimed at creating actual normative worlds based on the expression of the need for the desirable and the claim of something that should be. This prescriptive power is erected via the creation of a sort of community of consumers (from which it becomes difficult to escape); this is what seems to be put across by the series of T-shirts which, by way of successive relations of transitiveness, assert "We Are God," leaving behind some doubt as to the identity of the "we," which may, turn by turn, describe a single person (Starck?) or else everyone, or no one (the community of consumers thus founded) or even what is not yet someone (whence the re-emergence of the Annunciation theme).[27] The designer advances hidden and works his way surreptitiously into the object, like the binder in a sauce: "Looking at the object like a manifesto is suicidal, and sentences it to non-inclusion. You have to slip creation into the object like folding milk into a sauce, if you want to be able to talk to people." This notion of bond/binder is primordial because it underpins a religious metaphor, insofar as the implicit desire is here to bind people together between them (under the aegis of the community) and to bind these individuals to God (Starck?). This community endures, incidentally, through the sacrament of the communion, splendidly illustrated by OAO organic wine, which shows to what degree "we are what we eat."[28]

So, far from being an end in itself, the Starckian object ushers in a system of intercession, and metaphorical communion between a demiurge-designer and consumers, whose minds must be focused, by marking their bodies, on a certain number of ethical and aesthetic precepts. This marking, incidentally, is significant in the recurrence of the theme of tattooing (see, in particular, the photo of Starck tattooed with his objects and his slogans) or, alternatively, in a product like the cutaneous watch, as if the Starck spirit were literally incorporated in the minds and bodies of his consumers. There is a deification, not so much of Starck the man as of the Starck brand which, through its tremendous gift of being here, there and everywhere, can be applied to all objects; it operates like a kind of halo which incarnates objects and places, and imbues them with a spirit, a way of seeing the world, of acting, thinking and loving... as if by way of a phenomenon of trans-substantiation. So there is a certain magic but also possibly a mystique about the Starckian object, at once denigrated as a "non-object" and deified as essential, fundamental and consubstantial. This process calls to mind mystics who "punctuate their tales with the 'next-to-nothing' of sensations, encounters and daily tasks. The fundamental, for them, cannot be separated from the insignificant. This is what offers relief to the anodyne. Something is on the move in the humdrum. The mystic discourse turns detail into myth; it clings to it, it exaggerates it, it multiplies it, it deifies it."[29] Isn't this precisely what Philippe Starck attempts to design with objects and places?

Translated by Simon Pleasance

1. Sixth stanza of the *Spiritual Canticle* of St. John of the Cross quoted in Michel de Certeau, *La Fable mystique*, Paris, Gallimard, 1982, p. 14.
2. Quotation taken from François Dagognet, *L'Eloge de l'objet*, Paris, Vrin, 1989, p. 12.
3. We borrow the paratext idea from Gérard Genette, who defines it in a literary context as "the reinforcement and accompaniment of a certain number of productions, either verbal or otherwise, like an author's name, a title, a preface, illustrations [...] which [...] surround and prolong it, precisely in order to *present* it, in the usual sense of this verb, but also in the stronger sense: so as to *make it present*, to ensure its presence in the world, its 'reception' and its consumption." See Gérard Genette, *Seuils*, Paris, Seuil, 1987, p. 7. In this case in point, all the paratexts tally with the different textual layers which surround and legitimize the various Starckian productions: names of objects, legends, interviews, etc.
4. Quoted in Conway Lloyd Morgan, *Starck*, Paris, Adam Biro, 1999, p. 17.
5. Ibid., p. 11.
6. Ibid., p. 21.
7. The notion of legitimacy is incidentally a notion regarded as evident to explain the role of the contemporary designer: "The basic question is first and foremost that of the legitimacy [...] of asking oneself the question of the legitimacy of products to exist [...]. The legitimate act of the designer is firstly the matter about the legitimacy of the product, this is what gives it its real existence," in the Philippe Starck interview conducted by Elisabeth Laville pour the *Lettre d'Utopies*, August 15, 1998, p. 1.
8. Here is the complete Philippe Starck quote: "A toothbrush is 28 grams of matter, 28 francs to buy and it's made to get rid of scraps of meat from between the teeth. Every gram of matter must provide its service as best it can. My trade is to be a producer of fertile surprises, an opener of doors in people's heads..," in "Psychanalyse de l'objet Starck," *Le Monde*, January 27, 1994.
9. Quotations taken from the interview which Philippe Starck gave to *Marie-Claire Maison*, special issue, June 2001.
10. "The major challenge for a designer now consists above all in bringing happiness. By asking oneself questions about what is really missing in today's society: a sense of civic responsibility, love, compassion [..] good will replace beauty [...] instead of being useful, beauty will finally be able to blossom for the benefit of man alone...," excerpt from the interview given by Philippe Starck to the magazine *Elle*, on March 16, 1998.
11. Extract from the program in the Good Goods catalogue for La Redoute, 1998.
12. Ibid.
13. Ibid.
14. Quoted in C. L. Morgan, op.cit., p. 49.
15. As has incidentally been demonstrated by Christine Colin in "Bonne Marchandise. Good Goods or l'utopie en 8 T-shirts," in *design et utopies. Industries françaises de l'Ameublement. Les Villages 2000*, pp. 8-21. This utopian character of the project is incidentally thoroughly assumed by Stark, who defines himself as "an old daydreaming utopian communist hippie," in the interview given to *Elle Décoration*, no. 106, p. 182.
16. Christian Godin, *Faut-il réhabiliter l'utopie?*, Nantes, Pleins Feux, 2000, p. 10.

17. Françoise Choay, "L'utopie et le statut philosophique de l'espace Édifié," *Utopie. La Quête de la société idéale en Occident*. Exhibition catalogue, Paris, Bibliothèque nationale de France/Fayard, 2000, p. 338.

18. The semiotic square is a tool that helps to visualize the relations existing between the different terms of a semantic category. Let us consider the semantic axis "representation vs. construction." It is easy to see that these two terms form a semantic category in which each term presupposes the other through a relationship of contrariness. Just as structural semiotics starts from a simple principle which is that any system of signification is above all a system of relations, we then develop an interest in the different envisageable methods of the semantic category "representation/construction"; these two terms are linked by a relation of contrariness. In particular it is possible to envisage that relations other than just contrariness organize this semantic category. It is thus possible to envisage, through a system of negation, the contradictoriness of each one of these terms. "Non-representation" is the opposite of "representation"; "non-construction," for its part, contrasts with "construction." It thus becomes possible, with the help of these four terms, to represent a square, known as a semiotic square, which articulates the semantic category "representation-construction." This square sheds light on three types of relations:

- horizontal relations of contrariness: "representation" is the opposite of "construction" and "non-construction" is the opposite of "non-representation";
- diagonal relations of contradiction: "non-representation" is the contradiction of "representation" and "non-construction" is the contradiction of "construction";
- vertical relations of complementarity: in fact, "representation" turns out to be complementary to "non-construction" just as "non-representation" is complementary to "construction."

19. Arlette Barré-Despond (ed.), *Dictionnaire international des arts appliqués et du design*, Paris, Editions du Regard, 1996, p. 92.

20. Observations taken from "Le moins est le plus. Portrait de Martin Szekely," in *Libération*, October 18, 2000, p. 56.

21. This is the whole meaning of Andrea Branzi's sentence: "For people, building a house means making a place and objects with which it is possible to establish relations linked not only with their use and their functionality, but also relations of a psychological, symbolic, poetic nature," quoted in Alberto Alessi, *L'Usine des rêves. Alessi depuis 1921*, Cologne, Könemann, p. 64.

22. Quoted in Claude Deloffre, "Le Starck System," in *Marie-Claire Maison*, special issue, June 2001.

23. "The 9months T-shirts help women to show everyone how their child is developing inside their body."

24. Whence the question posed by Starck about Moosk: "Inanimate objects, do you have a soul?"

25. Extract from the Good Goods catalogue, op. cit.

26. Ibid.

27. Cf. Jean-Luc Nancy, "Conloquium," in Roberto Esposito, *Communitas. Origine et destin de la communauté*, Paris, PUF, 2000, p. 6.: "How are we to say 'we' other than as a 'one' (= everyone and no one) and other than an 'I' (= a single person, which is still no one...). So how are we to be in common without making what tradition [...] calls a community?"

28. "Man is an ecosystem in which the mind cannot be dissociated from the body and its food, in a relationship of interdependence. If it is widely admitted that food has an influence on the health of the body, it is nevertheless odd that we do not recognize its role in relation to thought."

29. M. de Certeau, *La Fable mystique*, op. cit., p. 19.

Valérie Guillaume

Reading and Un-reading the Object

Reading and un-reading the object. The reduplication of the title, which straightaway incorporates reflection in the refusal of over-simplifications, passes on a typical feature of the object created by Philippe Starck—its fable. Stripped of its usual name and requalified, the object actually takes part in a history, its own, the history of a man, his questioning and his thinking. This latter, in cheerful mood, has been wont to present "a word-related event in a thing-related guffaw of laughter,"[1] as is shown by one or two examples: Dr. Skud for a flyswatter, Boom Rang for a chair, Cicatrices de Lux for a lamp, Excalibur for a toilet brush, Dadada for a stool and so on. Described like a pure moment of jubilation,[2] inspiration dictates a memory, a dream or a game as its corollary. Effects of acoustic expressiveness are always carefully worked, as if their physical and emotional charge were a way of being freed from matter, and wrenched away from the object. In a different way, freedom and wrenching away signify resistance, tension, violence and death; creation features and achieves the complexity of man's relation to the world. But if reading Philippe Starck's design makes us face up to this kind of complexity, how are we to proceed? We know from experience that taking an object apart helps us to understand how it works. This is our intent. How does Philippe Starck work? The advantage of this close look at his method is that it in no way alters the ambiguous charm of the object. Becoming well acquainted with the design and making of the object also lends a greater sensitivity to powers than the distinctive mark of strangeness most often indicates. Strange, here, is this chair called Dr. Sonderbar—the German adjective used being translated into English as "strange," no less. Strange, there, is the vase called Quatre Étrangetés contre un mur. Formed by the emotions it arouses as well as by the images it offers, the feeling of strangeness sets the object within a masterful set, where Philippe Starck puts the finishing touches to all the angles of vision.[3]

I WORK ON MY OWN

> "*I work on my own, because the only pleasure I have is daydreaming, that kind of orgasm you have when you pick up a pencil, and a sheet of paper, and you have an intuition, and you see the thing taking shape...*"(1985).
>
> "*Personally speaking, I always live in a basic, isolated way [...]. I go on working on my own in a hut in the middle of a forest, watching the stags trot past...*"[...] (1993).
>
> "*I always live with someone, but I work on my own. The vibration of the other in work bothers me. For reasons to do with lack of self-confidence in relation to a potential dominant feature. [...] In my relation to the other, [...] I have trouble developing concepts*" (2000).[4]

If we look at these almost identical statements, uttered over a fifteen-year period, it is interesting to move closer to this unknown territory where creative inspiration looms up. Philippe Starck doggedly claims that he is living several lives at one and the same time, traveling from one house to another, and then, in each house, from one room to the next, as if he were a stranger to the places he lives in and—is this a consequence thereof?—presents. For the different

Cap-Ferret cabins, and those in Rambouillet forest or on the island of Formentera have been covered by photo reports in women's magazines. You get the impression that a mystery is not being pinned down because solitude is actually a non-place. The designer remains all the more elusive because he himself diagnoses the presence of a "magma" which is plastic and amorphous. Philippe Starck realizes inspiration like an emotional intensity.

What sticks with us about these different enigmatic realities is the tremendous energy potential which, in any hypothesis, presides over the creative act. A block of tracing paper and a pencil make up the designer's tool kit. No eraser. He prefers to filter or sieve rather than rub out. Put another way, he gradually overlays different sketches to use their outlines by way of transparency: "I draw... I move the sheet of paper underneath... What's left? This... That... Going through a filter is one of the parameters of the longevity of a creative act."[5] The doubling up of the sheet of paper encompasses additional creative processes, and facilitates an intense and condensed line of thinking helping to get rid of what is secondary, and focus on what is essential. Even body language, another motif: might doubling up also stem from decorative procedure? An example of this, for example, is the foyer of the Sanderson Hotel in London. Around the foyer, on white painted walls and on the front windows, two panels of white curtains are hung, with see-through glass wall lights and canine portraits between them. In the exercise of seducing the eye, doubling up (or surfacing) links two extreme graphic processes: blurring and separating, with dissimulation helping to reveal the essential and significant features.

At the heart of creation, drawing thus has a favored place; it plays a vector-like part, making it possible, initially, to be ahead of your closest associates—Bruno Borrione and Thierry Gaugain—and their teams, and then of manufacturers, craftsmen and industrialists. It is impossible to overstress the importance Philippe Starck then attaches to the intrinsic unity of the project,[6] as can be seen in various Thomson (1993-1998), OAO (since 1998) and Good Goods examples for the mail-order company La Redoute (1998) and Target (2002). He demonstrates an outstanding capacity for organizing distinct processes—materials, techniques and manufacturing processes, forms, colors, finishes, functional uses, qualities, packaging, how-to-use notices, brochures—by dint of an overall symbolic exactingness. A written text or oral commentary goes with each object or each architectural work, re-creating a context and lending a destiny to the object which, quite unlike the designer, cannot remain alone and silent. It has the task of interpreting the most diverse of pleas: thus "*the Aprilia Motó 6.5* is right. Two wheels, a fuel tank and an excellent engine. The motorbike is straightforward and friendly, and doesn't need to sport the useless and dangerous signs of machismo."[7]

I DON'T HAVE ANY CULTURE

"I don't have any culture"—a recurring leitmotiv.[8] The link between culture and memory, as we know, runs deep. If voluntary memory leads to a scholarly erudition from which Philippe Starck instinctually shies away, the affective memory of objects come across and observed, on the other hand, plus the memory of documents read, leads to culture. The designer here adds a personal ear to the expectations of whoever is making the commission and a painstaking examination of the way objects are used in practice.[9] Supposing that Philippe Starck's culture stems in effect from this particular form of memory, the brief listing made hereinafter takes into account, via successive chronological and geographical strata, the immensity of Starck's field of investigation.

What emerges from the history of furniture are thus objects, by turns reappraised and reinterpreted. Analogies have been noted between the work of Pierre Chareau produced in the 1930s and the formal options of the famous three-legged seats furnishing the Café Costes in Paris (1982): their rounded backs are one with the identical arms. Two areas of motivation hallmark the latest proposals. The first awakens the collective memory of "furniture's unconscious": nineteenth-century bathroom furniture, club chairs, rattan garden seats, utilitarian seats reproduced in English and American sales catalogues from the 1930s and 1950s, for example. In this regard, Starck declares: "It seems necessary to me to revisit the archetype of the small lamp that each one of us has also carried within us. This is Miss Sissi." The second shares the most eclectic recollections of our journeys, such as African stools, Indian wall lights and small figures, garden gnomes... Be it nostalgic or parodic, the dynamic echo of the reiteration crystallizes a new relation of objects with time and space. The evocation of their sexual ingredients and the appropriation of their social settings were inadmissible and uncommon prior to Starck.

From one or two Japanese and Italian designers, Philippe Starck has inherited a remarkable stylistic inventiveness, and a remarkable attentiveness to the script as well as to the symbolic detail.[10] Shiro Kuramata, for his part, possibly suggests to him the idea of weightlessness, and Toshiyuki Kita the quest for the object's flexibility.

The Italian Paolo Deganello combines his work as a whole with theoretical stances on design and, in particular, on its social function. The AEO[11] seat, dismantled and thoroughly examined by Philippe Starck, was the inspiration for the Neoz seats (1995). In 1995, it was precisely as a tribute to the Luminator[12] lamp by the Castiglioni brothers that Philippe Starck came up with the Rosy Angelis lamp (1994). The links of relatedness between Philippe Starck's and the Castiglionis' demonstrations are evident. They have a great deal in common: the use of the wall as a support for the tipped object, the study of all the possible ways of folding tables and chairs alike, the use of poor materials cobbled together with already existing forms, the desire to inventory and try everything.

Lastly, by making science-fiction his raw material, Philippe Starck takes cognizance of what it lends to the joint representation of erotic desire and angst. "There is a real assonance between Starck's morbid, even suicidal, view of the world, and Philip...Dick's brilliantly skewed vision of future worlds with its dark and absurd undertones and its elevation of objects to ritual vehicles of cult memory"[13]: the Juicy Salif lemon squeezer (1988) is the best example of this. The look of it calls to mind a three-legged gadget, at once threatening and intriguing, designed by the Belgian Edgar P. Jacobs in 1947 in *The War of the Worlds*.[14] For in order to exist fully, the object needs to interlock desire and fascination. Philippe Starck here suggests a key interaction, fantastic in essence, between human being and object: the eye is the basis of the object which, in return, alters it.

Like the American novelist, Philippe Starck does not talk about the future, but rather steps up the number of miniaturizing and magnifying effects. The objects in the exhibitions "Design français, 1960-1990" (Paris, Pompidou Center, 1988) and "Vanity Case by Starck" (Barcelona, 1991, and Moscow, 2002) reproduce real forms, and are miniaturized, whereas those placed in hotels are oversized.

As Claude Lévi-Strauss noted: “Unlike what happens when we try to get to know a thing or a person actual size, in the scaled-down world, knowledge of the whole precedes knowledge of the parts.”[15] Miniaturization thus causes the parts to disappear in a kind of hallucination of the whole. To this comment the Italian sociologist Pietro Bellasi adds that “the scale [and oversized] model comes about through the fragmentation of an external reality and then takes on a form of life that is altogether peculiar, separate and solitary, like its contracted double: in this sense, it is an autistic object.”[16] The author explains that the secret of the creation of such objects lies in the use of the comparative “more,” when it comes to describing them. Larger or smaller, they nevertheless come across as more real than the real.

“SONDERBAR,” OR: PERCEPTIBLE EXPRESSIONS OF STRANGENESS

The lines of force of Philippe Starck’s works may have already been analyzed, but only rarely have people developed any line of thinking in the area of the “perceptible,” in such a way, as is indicated by Georges Didi-Huberman, as to “launch a bridge between the double distance of the senses (the sensory senses, in this instance sight and touch) and meaning senses (semiotic senses, with their own equivocations and spacings).”[17] This praxis offers the pleasure—at least for anyone giving themselves over to it—of summoning up moments of quietness and gentleness, in the interval between tensions.

As a prime and brilliant commentator on his own work, Philippe Starck thus very precisely chalks up his most recurrent compositional features. Irregular trapezia, and diagonal and triangular lines all help to create dissymmetries and disjunctions as illustrated by the following examples. Many objects—lights and lamps (Easylight, 1979, Soudain le sol trembla, 1981, MacGee (1977), bookcases (John Ild, 1977), mirrors (Caadre, 1997-1998)—are propped obliquely against the wall, like so many flying buttresses in an exercise involving thrust. The balancing act of the three-legged seats (Costes, 1982; W.W., 1990) creates a tension. The arrangement of objects, and the way they are put together, obviously serve an aesthetics of conflict, which becomes perceptible as much in the graphic line as in the density. The clash between the solid foreground and the empty background of the Richard III armchair (designed for the Palais de l'Elysée [the French president's official residence] in 1981 and produced by Baleri in 1984), and between the plastic seat and the metal back of the Dr. Glob seats[18] (1985) and the Louis XX seats (1992), sets up the confrontation which, in principle, directs creative activity. "I arrived [at the Kartell company] making things of wood; I turned my back on plastic. To get plastic out of its ghetto I made with it what I could have made with wood. I actually only held on to two aspects—what can be moulded or cast, and what can be reproduced. I highlighted the sharp angles, and the planes..."

Similarly, and when he is designing hotel fixtures and fittings, and refurbishments, Philippe Starck uses the extremely diverse works of Gaudí, Alvar Aalto, Ray and Charles Eames, Eero Aarnio, Pierre Paulin, Marc Newson, Patrick Ghia, Jasper Morrison, Jurgen Bey for Droog Design and Ingo Maurer for the quality of their backward-turned enlightenment... as well as copies of a Louis XV marquetry wardrobe or a Jacob Desmalter armchair for Caroline Murat's silver room at the Elysée[19]... to put them within composite sets. Here, Philippe Starck makes an iconoclastic synthesis which challenges the current hierarchy drawn up between cultural references, mixing furniture that is popular, artisanal, industrial, design-related or rustic, original or copy. In using aesthetic processes involving collage and montage, the designer experiments with issues of "continuity, discontinuity, contiguousness, surplus, addendum, dearth, concealment, suture, pointing, unity and multiplicity, explosion and refocusing of the work, space, time, narrative, language [...]. This play area refers to a physical or mental activity which, in the consciousness of the person giving himself over to it, has just one goal: the pleasure it obtains."[20]

What is more, the monolithic and more or less apertureless configuration of stout volumes used by Philippe Starck encompasses an original process of internalization. For "it is really important here to accept division: [...] violence that cuts, splits, demolishes, propels [and] the solidity of a carapace, homogeneity and compactness."[21] Upside down, the envelope thus becomes the seat of sensibility. As in a shadow play, the way the eye works is rendered more complex by curtains filtering light, opalescent windows, weightless objects and, last of all, by the presentation of erasure (La Marie[22] and Louis Ghost, polycarbonate seats, 1998 and 2001). La Marie is a one-piece structure, apart from a rearmost piece of the seat itself which is inset using neither screws nor glue. The complete see-throughness of the chair is not obstructed by any ribs or struts, which, as analyzed by Philippe Starck, puts it "on the edge of total disappearance." In other respects, the control mechanisms are abandoned in favor of the gestural light touch which conditions the material environment as if by magic: the switches for the Soudain le sol trembla lamp (1981) and the prototype of the Ray Menta light (1984) have a digital contact; when the horn is tipped, the Ara light goes on or off (1988).

The light touch sets reflection in a more prominent position in the issue of the caress. This concept was introduced by the philosopher Emmanuel Levinas as follows: "The caress is a way of being of the subject, [...] what is caressed is not strictly speaking touched [...], the caress does not know what it is looking for. This 'not knowing,' this fundamental lack of coordination is its essence. It is like a game with something that slips away, and a game absolutely without any project or plan, not with what might become ours or us, but with something else, always different, always inaccessible, also to come. The caress is the expectation of this pure, content-free future. It is buoyed up on this growth of hunger, or invariably rich promises, opening up new avenues onto what is elusive and impalpable."[23] So the caress gets people to discover another kind of contact with the object, which is not merely capture, know-how and knowledge, but also encounter, relationship and experience—a kind of contact which confirms and demonstrates our present-day determination to achieve meta-sensoriality. Philippe Starck's recent work takes this into account with even more acuity. Consider, for example, the Alo digital telephone with voice recognition (1995), wrapped in elastic and see-through flesh, designed to be caressed rather than handled.[24]

Thinking about tactile sensibility, as applied by Philippe Starck to design, ordains a second sequence issuing from this exercise of the eye. Many photographic processes, in particular, hallmark the interior arrangements of hotels. Disproportionately elongated pieces of furniture (benches, sofas, tables), others (chairs and stools) that are evenly aligned, draw typical vanishing lines. When caught in a lens with a variable focal length, the object may be reduced, enlarged, over-sized, framed, and off-centered[25]... By borrowing already mentioned motifs (in particular, curtains and glass), and by adding to them processes which weaken the effects (matte and pastel[26]), Philippe Starck intentionally puts the onlooker in front of a blurred image. "The blurred image is distributed along three axes: what it is not (not clearly defined); the tactile impression it gives (softened); and the forms of thought it inspires (the vague, the indecisive and even the clouded)." In a persuasive demonstration, Serge Tisseron analyzes the contemporary forms of the advent of a blurred aesthetics which "[talking] the language of Epicurus: 'nothing dies, everything is transformed,' [...] catches time and assures us that we will also find the world different, otherwise put, always available to the desire which we project onto it [...]. [But] this form of anticipating the future development of the world does not have exclusively comforting aspects. It actually arouses the anxiety to do with the dissolution of the world and of our own erasure."[27] This is when Philippe Starck bursts out laughing—which is what we do, too.

Translated by Simon Pleasance

1. Pierre Fedida, *L'Absence*, Paris, Gallimard, 1978, p. 97. See also Gianni Vattimo, *La Société transparente*, Paris, Desclée de Brouwer, 1990, p.11. The author quotes this remark by Nietzsche: "In the end the real world becomes a fable."
2. Cf. Philippe Starck's observations collected by Brigitte Fitoussi in *Architecture d'Aujourd'hui*, no. 237, Feb. 1985, p. 86: "I'm an intuitive person. My first approach in terms of furniture also goes through a parenthesis in time, a siesta, for example, during which I dream, I imagine things. And it's often after a sudden flash that shoots across my mind that I start on a sketch. This is what I call the 'orgasm of creation' because the pleasure of inventing an object is the only interest I have in plying this trade [...]. Then I put this idea through a whole raft of requirements."
3. Dr. Sonderbar three-legged chair, 1983, produced by XO. *Quatre Étrangetés contre un mur* vase, 1987, produced by Daum from 1988 on. See also Louis Vax, *La séduction de l'Étrange* [1965], Paris, PUF, "Quadrige" series, 1967, p. 307.
4. Excerpts from interviews given by Philippe Starck to: Marc Breitman, in *Architecture Mouvement Continuité*, no. 7, March 1985, p. 26; Odile Fillion, "Philippe Starck, le juste produit," in *Modernité et Modestie*, Liège, Mardaga, 1993, pp. 54-56; and rushes from a documentary about Philippe Starck, made in 2002 by Pierre Doze.
5. Quotation taken from the film made by Catherine Terzieff and Célia Kendall, *Philippe Starck*, La Cinquième, Centre national pédagogique, "Design-Designers" series, 2001. See also the interview conducted by Christine Colin in *Jardin des Modes*, Dec. 1994-Jan. 1995, p. 38: "What interests me is getting down to it."
6. Cf. Author's interviews with Gérard Vergneaux and Elsa Francès, Paris, Thomson Multimedia, Sept. 2001; and with Philippe Woitrin, Paris, Limafood, OAO, Sept. 2001.
7. Philippe Starck in Good Goods.
8. "I have hardly any answers for value judgements, which are essentially cultural notions which I have trouble responding to because I don't have any

culture. I am not at all sure that this is the moment of culture, I think there are other more pressing emergencies." In *Philippe Starck: distordre*, edited by Marco Meneguzzo, Milan, Electa/Alessi, 1996, p. 47.

9. Cf. the remarks of the Bénéteau director as recorded by Carine Lenfant-Valère in *d'A, d'Architectures*, no. 85, July-Aug. 1998, p. 21: "[Philippe Starck] is not a designer, he's a sociologist. From 1977 on, our boats were made of teak. Starck pointed out to us that teak was a structural timber. He opted for mahogany, a cultural yachting species; he's happier using marble than Formica for working surfaces in kitchens, and advocates white fabric chairs."

10. Cf. Philippe Starck's remarks in *AA, L'Architecture d'Aujourd'hui*, n° 237, Feb. 1985, p. 86: "I've certainly got references, but they have to do with slightly blurred reminiscences. I don't have enough memory for them to dare to wittingly express themselves, and I'm naïve enough to work without references [...]. I don't have any precise references in mind. Rather, I've got attractions for architects like Gaudí, Mendelsohn, Aldo Rossi and Piano, and above all for the work of the designer Paolo Deganello. The Torso and AEO armchairs are the most significant objects of the period."

11. Paolo Deganello, born in 1940, is one of the founders of the Archizoom group. His AEO seat, produced by Cassina, dates from 1973, and the Torso seat from 1982. Cf. Claudia Neumann, "Cassina," in *Dictionnaire du design. Italie*, Paris, Éditions du Seuil, 1999, p. 181.

12. The *Luminator* light by Achille and Pier Giacomo Castiglioni, a 1955 project, made by Gilardi and Barzaghi, has been produced by Flos since 1994. Cf. Domitilla Dardi, *Achille Castiglioni*, Rome, Testo e Immagine, "Universale di Architettura" series, 2001, p. 27.

13. Cf. Conway Lloyd Morgan, *Starck*, Paris, Adam Biro, 1999, p. 74. the massive silhouette of the dinosaur Godzilla, hero of fantastic Japanese films of the 1950s and 1960s, inspired the architecture of the Nani Nani building. See C. Lloyd Morgan, op.cit., p.51; see also David le Breton, "Philip K. Dick, un contrebandier de la science-fiction," in *Esprit*, Oct. 1988, pp. 81-87.

14. *The War of the Worlds* (1898), science fiction novel by H.G. Wells illustrated by Jacobs in 1947.

15. Claude Lévi-Strauss, *la Pensée Sauvage*, Paris, Plon, 1961, p. 35.

16. See the article by Pietro Bellasi, "A propos du mouchoir de Gulliver. Essai sur l'imaginaire miniaturisant," in *Objets prétextes, objets manipulés*, texts compiled by Jacques Hainard and Roland Kaeht, Neuchâtel, Musée d'ethnographie, 1984, pp. 27-43.

17. Georges Didi-Huberman, *Ce que nous voyons, ce qui nous regarde*, Paris, les Éditions de Minuit, 1992, p. 125.

18. Dr. Glob chair, 1985, produced by Kartell from 1988 in a line of eight matte pastel colors. Cf. *La Donation Kartell. Un environnement plastique. 1949-1999*, Paris, Éditions du Centre Pompidou, "15x21" series, 2000, p. 74.

19. The reception room was appointed in 1807. The copy of the Jacob Desmalter armchair features in the foyer of the Sanderson Hotel in London. See *Connaissance des arts*, Apr. 1995, pp. 58-59.

20. *Rhétoriques des arts. Montages/Collages*, Pau, Université de Pau, second Cicada conference, Dec. 5-7, 1991, pp. 8, 154.

21. François Dagognet, *Philosophie d'un retournement*, Fougères, Encre marine, 2001, p. 48.

22. *La Donation Kartell...* op. cit., p. 86.

23. Emmanuel Levinas, *Le Temps et l'Autre*, Paris, PUF, "Quadrige" series, 1991, [4th ed.], pp. 82-83.

24. Alo is a "dream product" by the Tim-Thom team of Thomson Multimedia (concept: Philippe Starck; design and graphics: Jérôme Olivet). Voice-controlled telephone with technological node cast in polymer-enclosed aluminum alloy. See also Christine Colin, *Design et Utopies*, Paris, Ifa/Les Villages, 2000, p. 33.

25. Cf. Franco Bertoni's analysis, *Philippe Starck. L'architecture*. Liège, Mardaga, 1994, p. 34. Among the most recent examples we can mention: the Sanderson Hotel (London) with the *stretch* sofa in the foyer and the tall stools in the Long Bar, identically copying, on the rear of the back, the photograph of an eye by Ramak Fazel; the Mondrian Hotel (Los Angeles) with the table and thirty-six aligned chairs, all different. Cf. *Domus*, no. 794, June 1997, p. 59.

26. Philippe Starck uses three different color charts: French, Chinese and Japanese (DIC-Nippon), author's interview with T. Gaugain, Oct. 2001.

27. Serge Tisseron, "L'Avenir est dans le flou," *Petites Mythologies d'aujourd'hui*, Paris, Aubier, 2000. pp. 138-140. See also Marc-Alain Ouaknin, *Lire des Éclats. Eloge de la caresse*, Paris, Lieu commun, 1989, pp. 47, 52-54.

Sophie Trelcat

Architecture According to Philippe Starck

When asked how one should describe him, Philippe Starck responds that he is "someone who reveals the unconscious signs of society." Starck's response is telling of how much he is seeking to escape disciplinary frameworks and be free to embrace them all. Consequently, the point here is not to study a designer's architectural contribution, but rather to analyze a vision of architecture and its applications as forged by a creative mind, one who launches trends and sees the discipline as "a means of expression like any another."

This strategic distancing is essential to reading Starck's architectural work, which was and sometimes still is discredited by official architectural circles. It seems difficult to identify the key reason for this rejection: is it his laying claim to a natural genius humbly at the service of his contemporaries, or the demystification of architecture's hierarchical position by an outsider from the world of design? The question matters little, yet its possible responses shed light on both Starck as a personality and the state of architecture in the early 1980s. This period saw the birth of Starck's early projects, such as the entire architectural design of Les Bains-Douches (1978), the decoration and furnishing of the Palais de l'Elysée presidential apartments (1982-1984) and the design of Café Costes (1984). With just a few prominent interventions, Starck established an a-disciplined signature dedicated to conveying through space a lifestyle shared in an independent manner by a community of individuals. His architectural philosophy endured through the evolution of various trends, as is apparent in the hotels conceived for Ian Schrager two decades later.[1]

These cutting-edge concept-sites spring from an approach that makes a radical break with traditional architectural methods. From his earliest works, Starck was compared with the most innovative figures of the time, a period when theories of speed, the advent of home automation and the development of an "abstractive" minimalism aiming for purely visual and perceptual effects were revolutionizing architecture. The period also coincided with the development of computer-aided design, whose powerful impact on architecture's envelope and form is still a central issue today. The field subsequently underwent an identity crisis: postmodernism, with its references to classicism, grew stale, and traditional composition methods fell short when it came to a breed of architecture influenced by other fields of thought and contemporary artistic production . . . The positioning of someone like Starck within this transitional period indirectly coincided with the emergence of new points of reference, which revitalized architecture and urban design yet stopped short of actually constituting a structured avant-garde. In 1988, the exhibition *Deconstructivist Architecture*[2] brought together many of these groundbreaking figures. Mark Wigley, deputy curator of the exhibition, had this to say: "The disquiet these buildings produce is not merely perceptual; [. . .] What is being disturbed is a set of deeply entrenched cultural assumptions which underlie a certain vision of architecture." Working in the same spirit but from the sidelines, Starck plays up a relationship with architectural projects that is sentimental, even fantasy-oriented, underscoring affect over subject: "Architecture does not interest me, what interests me is creating fertile surprises."[3]

We sense a marketing logic behind this quest that is a legacy of the design world, yet also a desire for surroundings that generate emotions. According to Starck, the architect's mission is to rekindle our interest in the city. Deploring contemporary urban uniformity, Starck conceives architecture exclusively within the context of emotional urbanism and construes the city as a foundation for life, as a reservoir of emotions capable of supplanting notably television. He illustrated this urban utopia in 1991, in his one attempt at urbanism, the Rue Starck project, which is in fact partially realistic, as it integrates two existing buildings.[4] The Rue Starck project is composed of a series of autonomous buildings with strong semantic and communicative value, arranged on a checkerboard symbolizing a virtual, metaphysical site. Starck is conveying the vision of a future inter-communicating city, where physical movement is obsolete and techno-connected inhabitants wield a heightened sense of power. Traditional sites of urban scenery have been replaced by uncontrolled interstitial gray zones. Once again, Starck's dream-like intuition encounters the most prospective of architectural theories—the urban model and workings he depicts are reminiscent of the perfect zoning in Rem Koolhaas's Exodus project[5] and Andréa Branzi's analysis of our techno-informational ecosystem.[6]

Each of these conceptions of the city highlights the need for architecture to reposition itself; only a few of architecture's symbolic codes endure, given that one can live and work almost anywhere, on the condition of having access to the necessary facilities, services and information. With the Baron Vert,[7] Starck dares question the principle of opening up to the exterior. This disproportionate building with its blade-shaped profile is an imposing quasi-autistic jade mass. Yet each floor features a wide window obtained by a sort of horizontal scarification creating a series of deep slits in the facade, as if these sacrilegious openings were a remedy to its opacity. Functional but imperceptible from the exterior, these openings form a sort of one-way fenestration that heightens the building's visual impact. Many of Starck's building projects have exploited a minimum number of expressive means to achieve maximal effect by revolutionizing architectural codes, imposing the architectural object and creating a somewhat jarring effect within the urban landscape. The principle of incongruity meant to spark interest and amazement often prevails, as it does in the Tokyo building Nani Nani, an improbable silhouette whose name means "What is it?" or in the Asahi restaurant complex topped by a stylized monumental flame—imprinted in the minds of many of the locals. . . as a startling golden turd.

As a player who delights in playing with signs, Starck humorously manipulates both the objects' frame of reference and the appellations he bestows upon them. Whether it's a lemon squeezer or an office building, the result is always christened in a highly personalized manner. Thus the great Starck family grows, with all its branches borrowing from one another and quoting each other, as in Rue Starck; and it is sometimes difficult to map out a genealogy of influences. Scrambling all trails that do not lead back to him, Starck has an ambiguous relationship with the past and with potential architectural references. It might be tricky to sift through this issue with respect to this uncategorizable designer, who never attended architecture school. Yet it is tempting to cite the expressionism of Frank O. Gehry, who reformed the plasticity of architecture, as well as Aldo Rossi, who shares with Starck a theatrical language steeped in an obsession with time and death. Finally, while Starck claims to be interested in works like the Einstein Tower in Potsdam and in architects like Chareau, Mendini, Gaudí and Mendelsohn, his own works demonstrate an entirely different way of responding to the world and its transformations. Whether it is a product of oblivion or secrecy, the pathological amnesia with which Starck claims to be stricken emphasizes that he does not expect the past to help him face the present or the future.

"I forget therefore I am." This could be the declarative formula of this "weakness," claimed because it is a waiver, on which Starck leans to reinterpret forms and significations and to reify the symbols of society that he observes, anticipates and projects. As in touch with reality as he is with his nightmares, Starck attempts to, in the words of Franco Bertoni,[8] "persuade with new monsters." Take, for example, the small green zoomorphic monster Minato-Ku,[9] which could be kind of cute if it did not echo an image of a post-nuclear mutant, the impregnable citadels shaped like a high-powered armored car,[10] the facade resembling a shark's flank,[11] mirrors reflecting a deformed image of visitors,[12] protean masses inhabiting his projects . . . Philippe Starck's buildings are products of a mythology combining elements from both the collective and individual imagination. This architectonic bestiary-cum-sociological anthropology is bolstered by a mise en scène that is at times tormented, at times humorous, but always theatrical and often tragic. Starck's projects are like a multitude of scenarios employing tragedy as an extreme form of representation and narration and contributing to the formulation of his critical and introspective analysis of contemporary life. The author's personal myths become characters that the director aims to exorcise and transform into the collective heritage of an identifiable era. The central position of myth in Starck's architectural work joins up with the omnipresence of Starck himself as an object of representation and questioning within his work. There, too, the narcissistic aspect of the self-portrait coexists with a goal that goes beyond mere individuality—that of implementing architecture "as a description of things and of ourselves."[13] Egocentric yet working on behalf of the community, Starck sifts through the "I" in order to reveal the "we," yet avoids the pitfall of self-celebration by cultivating in his works self-derision, natural empathy, a sophisticated form of generous naïveté and the fragile humanity of existence, eternally divided between optimism and pessimism.

These characteristics imbue the provocative aspect of Starckian postures with ambiguity, and have undoubtedly contributed to this maverick's vision rarely being taken seriously. His nonstandard, theatrical and quirky proposals are often too quickly idolized or branded opportunistic and rebuffed; their critical and visionary pertinence thus becomes secondary. The reaction to the 1993 Trois Suisses catalogue campaign[14] illustrates this well: indeed, the scope of the idea, which offered an original way of thinking about the design and promotion of individual housing,[15] was completely underestimated. Stimulated by this focus on intimacy, Starck combines a high level of comfort with the most contemporary spatial norms in his house: each feature represents an alternative to the depersonalized world of tract housing (a personalized concept rather than "turnkey" and without identity; open, adaptable spaces rather than a sclerotic layout; a work modifiable into differentiated multiples rather than an industrial reproduction of a single model; exacerbated artifice in exoticism—a Canadian log cabin, a Chinese pagoda and a New York loft all in one—rather than fake regionalist authenticity). Finally, in hooking up with a specialist in mail-order selling, Starck endows his architectural vision with a veritable direct-marketing strategy.[16] The alliance startles and disturbs: the project seeks to reconcile high architecture with mass accessibility and, here again, constitutes an alternative critique to the undifferentiated catalogues of houses promoted by traditional developers. In this sense, Starck signs a sort of manifesto authenticated by his own experience,[17] and provides another example of this proselytizing Narcissus, who is at one with his public and campaigning for collective comfort; the house is presented as if it were Starck's own house, designed so that everyone can invent his or her own home on the basis of the example pictured and tested out by its creator.

Activist works deployed on all fronts of a "taste war," Starck's creations blend projection of our contemporary deviations with anticipation of positive evolutions. In counterpoint to his pessimism, Starck has faith in progress and likes to stimulate mutations through a multiform production—a prospective that startles just as propaganda does. Even more than a star, Starck is a brand serving his own vision. Everything about Starck competes to sustain our desire to consume his world—polished communications strategies, revitalization of image, games of absence and reappearance in the media sustaining mystery, audience and celebrity . . .. Impossible to reduce to a simple mercantile or narcissistic advertising campaign, this brand logic is also present in his approach to architectural design, focusing on the elaboration of a concept and the conditions that make it feasible. Starck has a knack for surrounding himself with the right people and steers clear of all technical management, which he delegates to a reduced, discreet team, entirely devoted to the brand. On another level, the transfer of part of his architectural activity to Japan suggests the need for an exceptional context for prospective projects, and allows his work to benefit from our fascination with the exotic. Fueling itself with the contexts it celebrates as well as those it transgresses, the Starck brand expands by serving other brands in a symbiotic relationship of promotional exchange. Such was the case for the Asahi building, of which the publication of sketches sufficed to make Asahi rise on the stock market, as well as the Laguiole factory crowned by a gigantic blade, making the product itself the most efficient sign for the brand.

Finally, the Starck brand also distinguishes itself by its recurrent vocabulary, which functions like an identifying code and a carrier of discourse, a logotype multiplied on the scale of a polysemic formal universe by which the author communicates *himself* and in which the public projects *itself*. Exacerbated to the point of expressionism, Starck's architectural vocabulary pushes the user into the position of actor, forcing him or her into a dynamic relationship with the buildings. The theatricality of the formal and functional mise en scène not only serves the building's aesthetic but also the ergonomics of climbing stairs,[18] moving about on checkered patterns,[19] raising curtains,[20] passing through and distortion of scale,[21] interacting with form or color . . . According to Starck, architecture is a formal and sensorial equation, experienced as a physical and emotional adventure that aims to perturb the user by arousing an interest for the movement taking place. Beyond fulfilling function, it sets off a new presence of architecture that is not entirely removed from the one envisaged by the deconstructivist architect Peter Eisenman[22] or the architectural principles borne by Wittgenstein's house.[23] This task of bringing together architecture and its user counterbalances the general dematerialization stipulated by today's world. When faced with a habitable space crossed over by uninterrupted fluxes of information and compromised by the processes of industrialization and consumerism, Starck attempts to give meaning to our new relationship to the artificial world. Thus, the architectural product of the Starck label can be defined as a "collective that has come to terms with individuality," in which our bodies are represented by transceivers, in which architecture transforms into an advertising medium, and in which the city acts out the metropolitan play.

Translated by Elizabeth Jian-Xing Too

1. For the more recent hotels: St. Martin's Lane (London, 1999), Sanderson (London, 2000), Clift (San Francisco, 2001), Hudson (New York, 2001), veritable "resorts" where housing and dining become an art de vivre for extravagant nomads.

2. An exhibition presented at MOMA, June 23 to August 30, 1988. It brought together several international architects who, at the time, were not well-known but are now major references in contemporary architecture: Coop Himmelb(l)au, Peter Eisenman, Zaha Hadid, Rem Koolhaas, Daniel Libeskind, Frank O. Gehry and Bernard Tschumi.

3. Franco Bertoni, *Philippe Starck. L'architecture* (Liège: Mardaga, 1994), p. 118.

4. Conceived as a development occupying part of Île Saint-Germain, where Starck had already built a private house (the Le Moult House, 1987), which was integrated into Rue Starck, as was a yellow replica of the Asahi building, built in Japan in 1990.

5. Dominique Rouillard, "Rem Koolhaas, Elia Zenghelis. Exodus ou les prisonniers volontaires de l'architecture, 1972," in *La ville, art et architecture en Europe, 1870-1993*, ed. Jean Dethier and Alain Guiheux (Paris: Centre Pompidou, 1994), pp. 436-437. Theoretical project on the city.

6. "We live in a megasystem of pieces of furniture, a gigantic lightscape, a wired territory that connects an infinite number of terminals, like an equalizing interface with artificial divisions, crossed over by tunnels of information and signs that have nothing to do with architecture," in Andrea Branzi, *Nouvelles de la métropole froide*, Les Essais (Paris: Centre Pompidou, 1991), p. 27.

7. Office building in Osaka (1990).

8. Bertoni, op. cit.

9. Nani Nani in Tokyo (1989).

10. Tower in Paris (1992).

11. The Baron Vert in Osaka (1990).

12. In the Paramount Hotel in New York (1990).

13. Aldo Rossi, *Autobiographie scientifique*, (Marseille: Parenthèses, 1988)./ Aldo Rossi, *A Scientific Autobiography* (Cambridge, Mass.: MIT Press, 1981).

14. In its line of designer products, the famed French mail-order store offered an "architect's house" on the inside of its catalogue's back cover (1993). Intended to bring together proposals by several architects (including Jean Nouvel and Frank O. Gehry), only the Starck House came to fruition. The kit sold by mail order contained plans for the house and a series of objects symbolizing the labor of building a house. The campaign received considerable media attention and counts several on-site realizations.

15. Undoubtedly, this will also be the case for his latest constructions underway (two residential high rises in Tel Aviv, a hotel in Rio de Janeiro, an

apartment building in Miami, another in Melbourne and the Taschen store in Los Angeles), regarding the urban planning of residential apartment buildings.

16. This type of alliance was renewed with La Redoute, on the terrain of everyday consumer goods (the Good Goods catalogue, 1998).

17. He stated in an interview with Frédéric Edelman in *Le Monde*, January 27, 1994: "I based my house on the pillow . . . simplicity and comfort . . ."

18. See the Le Moult and Formentera Houses, the Asahi building, Moondog . . .

19. See the Moondog building, the Mercedes building, the La Cigale concert hall, the Laguiole factory, Rue Starck . . .

20. See the Groningen Museum in the Netherlands and various hotels and restaurants.

21. See the French pavilion at the Venice Biennial, as well as the giant taquets and the deformed columns of the Asahi building.

22. "I look for ways to conceptualize a space that would place the subject in a shifted relationship, for [the forms] will no longer make iconographic references to the traditional forms of organization. . . . in order to ensure that people's relationship to architecture becomes less utilitarian." Peter Eisenman, in Philip Jodidio, *Formes nouvelles, architecture des années 90*, (Cologne, Lisbon, Paris: Taschen, 1997).

23. See, in particular, note 8: "The house in motion refers to the house in use. Use is not functionality (the path between sink and stove). Use is action such as opening a door, interlocking window-doors or raising metal curtains," and in note 15: "All of the materials are 'artificial' or 'unnatural.' . . . Despite his purely artificial material idiom, Wittgenstein succeeds in lending his architecture a high degree of sensuality and warmth." Bernhard Leitner, *The Wittgenstein House*, (New York: Princeton Architectural Press, 2000).

Christine Colin

Starck and France: Does Starck Have a Following?

"-ubique. It means...
- Everywhere, Joe said[1]

The question which this essay has been asked to answer may seem odd in the eyes of a declared "citizen of the world," doubling as a well-established individualist. And yet the matter of linkage to place and group that informs his work introduces us fairly and squarely to the nub of one of the most significant contemporary problem sets.

NOWHERE: NON-PLACES (PASSAGES, DECOYS, U-TOPIA)

Just as trees are sculpted by prevailing winds, does the shape of an object likewise betray features of territory, along with its geography and spirit-of-place? Is the shape of an object still part and parcel of the territory producing it, the way vines draw their savor from the earth?
A priori, everything about Starck's work seems to shift away from a place embodying the idea of permanence, such as a local area which fashions and

identifies the group of people "dwelling" therein, as well as the things they produce. In many respects, Philippe Starck is the typical "passenger" in "non-places" as described by Marc Augé: "Non-places are as much installations necessary for the sped-up circulation of people and goods (fast lanes, cloverleaf interchanges, airports) as actual forms of transport, or large shopping malls, or, again, extended transit camps where the planet's refugees are offloaded."[2]

Starck is a passenger in more than one sense. In a personal way: "As soon as I was old enough to take an airplane, I was there."[3] In a family way: "I'm a typical example of the rush to go West. My base is Russia, I must be Estonian or something like that, then I became German, thankfully not for long, and I moved through eastern France and reached Paris, which I used as a springboard to venture out into the world, with an important stepping stone in America. My French vision will always pass through the filter of the melancholy of the East. France doesn't exist per se, its wealth resides solely in the fact that it is a crossroads for immigrants. It has always only ever lived through passing foreigners." [4] And then in a "technical" way: "Technically I'm stateless. There are for certain reasons very precise accounts which show that I am no longer nowhere. I'm counting the days not to be American. I'm altogether a citizen of the world, and always have been. In passing this makes me indisputably European."[5]

Last of all, as a designer, Starck chose a non-place here, too—through the complete and radical impasse he had with French industry, preferring, in this terrain, mass distribution. In so doing—and the Good Goods catalogue he produced in 1998 for the La Redoute mail-order company is a manifesto of this—he is situated not on the side of the product (and its manufacture), which we may actually conceive of as still incorporated within the territory, but on the side of merchandise (Good Goods) and its distribution, which traces an abstract, homogeneous territory: the single Market. We'll come back to this.

EVERYWHERE: UBIK

Everything conspires to suggest that designer Starck was born not in France but in "Science Fiction," with *Ubik*,[6] the novel by Philip K. Dick (1969). Wasn't one of his first gestures to call his company "Ubik," and then give all his works dating from the early 1980s the names of characters from this novel? As the preface writer observes, *Ubik* is not easy to sum up in so many words, because of the complexity of the space-time framework. The world presented in it is prey to the most absolute kind of doubt. The borderline between life and death is itself uncertain because the living can turn to those who are half-alive and kept in "moratoria." Most of the places in which the characters grow are subject to a "temporal degeneration," which inexorably makes the objects found there retreat in time. The characters have to make extraordinary efforts to know where they are and when they are there. In the final analysis, most of the places turn out to be decoys produced by Jory's imaginative power—Jory being a half-alive teenager who plays cruel games, and leads his fellow creatures into them before consuming what life is left in them. In tandem with the loss of any sense of reality in these places, the novel describes a space-time factor entirely fashioned by merchandise, Universal Merchandise: Ubik. The advertising gimmicks at the beginning of each chapter appear curiously like the most tangible signs of the unreality to which science fiction introduces us: "Ubik is the nation's number-one choice in beer"; "New miracle Ubik, the easy-to-apply, extra-shiny, non-stick plastic coating"; "Instant Ubik has all the fresh flavor of just-brewed drip coffee"; "Ubik's self-winding Swiss chromium never-ending blade;" Ubik the revitalizing cream, the deodorant spray, the sleeping pill, the toothpaste and, last of all, the aerosol spray which will save the head of Rucinter Associates, a protection agency, and give him everlasting life.

So, far from embodying permanence and representing the supreme point of reference, because of its center, the place is, on the contrary, the favorite prey of illusion. Philippe Starck's Paris restaurant Bon seems like something straight out of this ghostly world. Like ectoplasm, it conjures up a literally bloodless world, one that is as if freeze-dried, devoid of flesh and matter, and, in the end of the day, stripped of reality. "Illusion? That's my specialty," Starck admits. "All my hotels are inspired by it. My latest hotel which opened in San Francisco is totally based on optical illusion, with things that are either too big or too small, pictures which move, wooden walls which turn into trees and forests. Things that aren't normal. This is the only thing that I find fun. It's my Grévin museum side[6a]—House of Miracles, Hall of Mirrors stuff. Everything is just illusion. Places which correspond to real life have to be an illusion. I'm forever trying to express general relativity. Some of my colleagues, with their solid wood, display an alarming lack of intuition about what real life truly is, and about the laws of physics. When you know that the stars you can see usually died billions of light years ago, you realize that nothing is true or real, not even the great eternal sky. A minimum of knowledge about physics shows that this corian tray, this mobile phone and my thumb are all made with the same molecules, which are activated in different ways. Love, the vibration between two people, is the only thing that brings you close to reality. The rest doesn't exist. I've never been close to reality. Beyond things passionate, I disintegrate in the molecules surrounding me."[7]

UNIQUE (PENDING THE INDEPENDENCE OF THE ILE-DE-FRANCE)

> *"Current events and the urgency of the present moment reign here.*
> *The passenger in non-places only finds his identity at the customs post,*
> *the motorway toll and the cash register."*[8]

"Never," in Marc Augé's words, "have the references of collective identification been so fluctuating," and never has the temptation to make reference to just the individual been so great. Philippe Starck echoes this "world promised to solitary individuality," as described by Marc Augé, without a moment's hesitation: "I'm viscerally independent, and a loner. I can only work on my own. I have a total resistance to team work, and things collective. I've muddied any chance I might have had to join up with a movement, and I've even scuppered any chance of a movement forming around me. I've always been something of a letdown, sending out misinterpretations and scuttling this, that and the other to avoid having anything whatsoever around me, precisely because I saw all that as being fraught with danger. I'm against global movements. A good idea snapped up by a movement prompts a fashion, and fashion leads to unfashionableness and the end of that idea."[9]

Starck may admit to a certain curiosity for the Italian "magma," but on the other hand he denies any link-up with any French design and with all offshoots thereof. Even in terms of science fiction, he acknowledges no kinship with Olivier Mourgue, who was in one of the scenes of *2001: A Space Odyssey*: "Mourgue doesn't feature in the interesting part of the film. He's made an object of modern style employed in a modern place as a modern object, and so for his naïveté. The interesting part of the film is the last scene which unfolds in a pale green apartment, evoking a kind of paradise, with the cultural shock produced by a Louis XV salon as if turned inside out by the luminous floor."[10] It is to this last scene that Starck refers: to that "collective memory as seen by P. K. Dick and Kubrick, and as if fossilized by modern technology."[11]

Just as the previous generation of French designers had felt no need to distance themselves from the overall Anglo-Saxon design model, so Starck and his successors have felt no need to distance themselves from the Italian situation, which encompasses the past twenty-five years of European design. Quite to the contrary, their sole aim was and has been to join these trends and play an active part in them. This makes it unlikely that any school will emerge, whatever the quality of the leading figures in French design, past and present alike. What lingers is a feeling of regret and nostalgia. The exhibition "Starck's Grandchildren?", which brought together former "assistants to the master," was, to say the least, not very affirmative, starting with the title.

The assembly of "former associates" of the agency suggests not so much a school as a Renaissance painting workshop, where the master gathered varying skills about him: the flower specialist, the landscape expert, the painter of animals and hands and so on. It outlines a jigsaw puzzle where you can find Starck's character traits: analytical capacity, ambition, a sense of site management, boastfulness, designs in space, mastery of words, a sense of what's topical, etc. The only thing that seems to bind them together is professionalism: "I have a bad professional conscience," Starck says. "I'm a Chinese painter."[12]

Christophe Pillet, who put together the interviews in the exhibition catalogue,[13] observes that he felt indebted first and foremost to Starck for having freed design from "gray-shirted industrial aesthetics [and for having] showed him the ins and outs of the star system and its success-related myths" (to which we should add the adjective "individual"). The 1980s actually witnessed the end of much of what, in design, came from the legacy of the two postwar periods (the Bauhaus and the Ulm High School for Design) and, with it, the end of a design more or less consolidated around the collective reconstruction project, which twice galvanized Europe in the twentieth century. In tandem, those particular years were the arena, in France, of a radical shift in the development and promotion of design. While specialized magazines lost their virtual monopoly, the general press accommodated designers under the "people" heading. From then on they were isolated in their "career," and identified just by their CV. This was a revolution that was far more important than it looked. Not so very long ago, Italian designers, in particular, were worried that a solo show might hasten them prematurely to the grave. The individual monograph, which used to be regarded as a more specifically commemorative and museum-bound genre, now forges the professional identity of contemporary designers, as soon as they leave college. In *Ubik*, this also conjures up the extraordinary and terrifying message—"I'm alive and you're dead"—that Rucinter sent to the members of his team, who thought he was dead, and they alive.

When he agrees to emerge from his proud individualism, the only group Starck makes reference to, and not unwittily, is his "tribe," wholly under the aegis of membership. Like the "studio" or "workshop," the tribe sketches a portrait of Starck in the form of a puzzle: "My fiancée, [...] my photographer, [...] my right arm, [...] my publisher, [...] my Italian, my doctor, my old buddy, my daughter, my electronic brain, not forgetting... *myself*."[14]

GENESIS, MYTH, INFORMATION

None of this, needless to say, would be of any particular interest if Starck talked not only a lot about himself, but also, in passing, about the genesis of the forms surrounding us, and more specifically the forms of objects.

We've all seen potters hoisting up their clay, and we've all had a chance to admire the extraordinary interaction between the tool, the object produced and its function. But who, nowadays, has ever seen the manufacture of a plastic chair, a radio or an industrial carpet? It has to be said that, by depriving craftsmen of their tools, the capitalization of the production tool has also deprived all and sundry of the visibility of the manufacturing process. Within an industrial context, with new materials and new technologies, designers in the Modern Movement desperately tried to put their fingers on that "traceability," that limpidity of the genesis of forms and the meaning of its process. Aphorisms like: "The tool creates the work" and "Form follows function" point to the extremely lowly place that modern designers allotted themselves in the genesis of forms. More than inventors, they set themselves up as observers, as witnesses of the process, and as trustees of its visibility. There can be little doubt that Starck is part of this line of "informer" designers. Like the great designers of the past twenty years, such as Castiglioni, Sottsass, Mendini and Mari, he informs us about the extremely complex, split and mysterious processes from which contemporary forms issue.[15] Like all informers, like it or not, he is simultaneously within and without, perforce a traitor. Like Archizoom and Superstudio, whose radical manifestos verge on a caricature of the characteristics of industry and mass distribution (in the alleged hope of precipitating their end), he is at once critical, up-in-arms and proselytical: an extremist. Just as modern designers forged the industrial myth, so postmodern designers are designing the commercial myth, in other words the narrative of the birth of a world based on commerce and trade. Archizoom's *No-Stop City* (1969), their most famous manifesto, presents a city shaped like a supermarket: a homogeneous and "catatonic" territory, to borrow an Andrea Branzi expression.

"Good Goods," for which the Good Goods catalogue is also the manifesto, can have no territory other than *No-Stop City*, the city without limits. These Good Goods, as announced in the catalogue's preface, are "non-objects": they are even "non-created," if we are to believe the label "No Creation No Chemical." This, a fortiori, does away with the question of their place of origin. The form of the object is an "archetype,"[16] which is to mass distribution what the standard is to mass production: a universalist ideal.[17] Having reached this point in history, after the appearance of so many divine attributes—ubiquity, uniqueness, universality—we won't be particularly taken aback to see God himself twice referred to on *political T-shirts* bearing Starck aphorisms in the Good Goods catalogue: "We are God" and "God is dangerous." These two sentences added to the title of the catalogue, "Good Goods," invite the exercise of logic and associations of ideas. If the choice of English is here reserved for God, is this not to make the most of the extraordinary likeness offered by the English language between the deity and goods? And, taking this superb alliteration that links goods and good a step further, all that is missing is one letter to give us goods—"We are goods"—or "God Goods."

"I am Ubik.
Before the universe was, I am.
I made the suns,
I made the Worlds.
I created the lives and the places they inhabit; I moved them there, I put them there.
They go as I say, they do as I tell them.
I am the world and my name is never spoken, the name which no one knows.
I am called Ubik, but that is not my name.
I am.
I shall always be.[18]

Starck ushers us into a world where the issue of the relationship between territory and product is not done away with, as we might be led to think by some of what goes before, but in reverse, as in the last scene of *Ubik*. For this very Kubrick-like reversal, as is also suggested by *No-Stop City*, it is no longer the territory that forms the product, but the goods which form, or more accurately "format," the territory and those living in it. Good Goods identify "citizen consumers."[19] And Starck's entry into politics,[20] no matter how whacky it might seem, may well have no other purpose than to get us to realize (or believe) that, henceforth, there is no other city than the one emerging from this extraordinary reversal.
From time immemorial, people have generally wanted to see in the form of objects, over and above their function, a reflection of the forces contributing to

their genesis. What are the forces present which decide on the form of objects? And even more so, what is the strength, the predominant value, the value which, beyond the host of influences and restrictions, will mark the form of the object with its seal? Ever since "God is dead," he who created the world in his image, in particular, has forever been looking for the image of whom and what the world of objects is formed. What is the design here?

Translated by Simon Pleasance

1. Philip Kindred Dick, *Ubik* [1969].
2. Marc Augé, *Non-lieux, Introduction à une anthropologie de la surmodernité*, Paris, Le Seuil, "La Librairie du XXe siècle" series, 1992.
3. Interview with Philippe Starck conducted by the author in September 2001, specifically for this new article.
4. Ibid.
5. Ibid.
6. P. K. Dick, *Ubik*, op. cit.

6a. The waxworks museum in Paris, equivalent of London's Madame Tussaud's, named after Alfred Grèvin [1827-1892], an artist renowned for his caricaturist drawings.

7. Interview, fn. 3.
8. M. Augé, op. cit.
9. Interview, fn. 3.
10. Ibid.
11. The fact remains that if we are to identify the main thread in these last three generations of French designers, it would undoubtedly be science fiction, as seems also to be the case with the "LuxLab" projects of Jouin, Gauguin and Massaud, or the latest Bouroullec brothers projects. But on what stage?
12. Interview fn. 3.
13. Pascale Cassagnau, Christophe Pillet, *Bref, Brétillot-Valette, Matali Crasset, Patrick Jouin, Jean-Marie Massaud. Petits-enfants de Starck?* Paris, Dis Voir, 1999.
14. Simone Philippi (ed.), *Starck, Cologne/Lisbon/ Paris*, Taschen, 1996.
15. Christine Colin (ed.), *L'Origine des gammes, Design et games, les Villages*, Paris, Editions Industries françaises de l'ameublement/Hazan, 2001.
16. Joe Ship, the hero of *Ubik*, wonders: "Perhaps this weirdly verified a discarded ancient philosophy, that of Plato's idea objects, the universals which, in each class, were real. The form *TV set* had been a template imposed as successor to other templates, like the procession of frames in a movie sequence. Prior reforms, he reflected, must carry on an invisible, residual life in every object. The past is latent, is submerged, but still there, capable of rising to the surface once the later imprinting unfortunately—and against ordinary experience—vanishes."
17. Christine Colin (ed.), *L'archétype est un songe, Objets-types et archétypes, les Villages*, Paris, 1997.
18. P. K. Dick, op.cit.
19. Good Goods catalogue, Lille, La Redoute, 1998.
20. See the interview referred to in fn.3 "For me, this exhibition is a balance sheet that I would like to be critical, and for once expressing what I have always non-said. The way I've wanted to piss off the rich, the way I've wanted to piss off institutions, and bad food. I'm an irritator. I'd like to show my rebellious targets. I've got enemies who've been there forever, the representation of money, luxury, oppression, fascism, machismo, inelegance, phoney products, phoney prices..."

Vanni Pasca

The Italian Period in the Work of Philippe Starck

Starck began working with Italian firms in 1984; for a decade, if not longer, this collaboration proved a decisive point that was to internationally associate his name with those companies. Schematically, the first period in Starck's work corresponds to his interior design of François Mitterrand's apartments at the Palais de l'Elysée and of Parisian nightclubs. The current period of his work has found expression for quite some time now in projects of collective, complex spaces that actually stage postmodernity; and, at the same time, in the pursuit—at least that is the claim—of utopia for the masses, something dear to the modern movement and which Starck wishes to reformulate today. But the phase of most central importance seems to be the one between these two periods, the "Italian period," which is the present focus.

I met Starck in 1984, in the company of the Italian industrialist Enrico Baleri, at the Milan airport. He wore an Issey Miyake jacket and a pair of jeans so ripped up they could not go unnoticed (this look was not yet very popular in Italy). He opened a metal attaché case on a table in a bar and took out some portfolios containing everything that magazines and newspapers around the world had published about him; held inside the lid of the case by elastics were sheets of blank paper, pencils and triangles. In sum, his trendy appearance was paired with a declaration of immediate availability—he was the complete opposite of the typical Milanese designer-architect of the time. More than an intellectual designer (like the Italian designer who is heir to the Bauhaus tradition), Starck came across as a professional who had no intentions of playing second fiddle. Even back then, he liked to proclaim himself an autodidact and let everyone know that he hated intellectuals, particularly because they tend to talk about design in "cultural" terms. All this suggested a new approach to both design and the image of the designer.

During the 1980s, many Italian firms undertook the development of new strategies. Indeed, it did not seem likely that their success in yesterday's national market would carry over to the future; moreover, they needed to launch into the conquest of other markets to maintain their objectives for expansion. However, in the 1970s and early 1980s, a new scenario was taking shape. In Italy, "new design" or postmodern groups like Memphis and Alchimia emerged while the experimental legacy of the radical movement was still full of potential. Paolo Portoghesi captured everyone's attention at the 1980 Venice Biennial with *Strada Novissima*, whose facades, designed by postmodern architects already known for their "scandalous," anti-rational buildings, were very well received by all, including the unspecialized press. Thus many firms became interested in designers considered "postmodern," on the condition that they had a strong and recognizable identity. In addition, they were keenly aware how advantageous it was to break into foreign markets via products conceived by designers who already had local renown.

At the time, Starck was a designer from France, a country reputed to have little sense of design. He was famous for his interior design of President Mitterrand's residence in 1982; he was also known as the author of two nightclub projects, La Main Bleue and Les Bains-Douches, whose decors reflect a distinctly metropolitan kind of brutality. Then came the success of Café Costes, whose design was in perfect sync with its clientele, and it appeared that Starck may well have created a "new generation" of interiors.

In fact, the problem Italian firms were then encountering was that the rather exuberant postmodern design of the early 1980s did not go with a concrete transformation of daily life in Italy. In the 1950s and 1960s, the economic boom had set off a modernization process that changed lifestyles profoundly, and electrical appliances (refrigerators, televisions, etc.) as well as modern interior designs made their entry into Italian homes. Inversely, in the 1980s, the success of "new design" remained a success of image, which, at best, occupied magazine pages, but did not find any real potential on the market.

Italian postmodernism had replaced asceticism with exuberance; thickness and profundity with slenderness and refinement; sobriety with colors and decoration; and composition with de-structuralization; it had also tried to re-establish a relationship with history (but entering this subject would lead to a different discussion). After all is said and done, we were in the presence of reversed "narratives," which opposed modern discourse but nevertheless remained narratives. Starck, on the other hand, was to go about it completely differently: he opted for a practice founded on stylistic eclecticism, going from communicating through discourse to communicating with images, playing on immediacy instead of depth of reflection, and developing mechanisms of signification powered by the object's iconic charge. While the experiment led by Italian firms with postmodern designers came to a dismal end from a commercial point of view, Starck was to make the sales of his objects soar.

Attentive to the success of Café Costes, Driade contacted the French designer because they felt he would be capable of establishing a relationship between layout and decor, and of designing furniture that matches up to a new sensitivity to collective or domestic spaces. Café Costes demonstrates a clever play of tension between the metal joists, which accentuate the separation between the two floors, the smoothness of the wall and floor surfaces, and the "decorative" grace of the steel balls placed between the pillars and the intrados of the staircase. The same element of tension is at work in the small three-legged armchair, whose fundamental metal structure is added onto a strong, welcoming and enveloping back. The relationship between modern "essentiality" and "decorative" elegance recalls the great Pierre Chareau and his capacity to combine the elegant effects of suppleness with the hardness of metal—somewhere between "decorative" tradition and the language of modernity. And this direction, which Starck carefully thought through, was to be marked by success: Driade still produces several of his designs, notably the J. (Série Lang) armchair and the M. (Série Lang) tables, and the furniture in the Royalton Hotel; Cassina more recently featured his beds and big divans. Meanwhile, in the late 1980s, other firms like Flos and Kartell got in contact with Starck, who thus enlarged the range of projects to which he applied his talent.

Together with elegance, Starck was also working on what we could call the object's "displacement." In the case of the Président M table, for example (produced by Baleri, but conceived for François Mitterrand's study in 1984), its technical precision, which is evident if we look at the dismantled parts composing this table, slips in other meanings: the inclined tubular feet constitute a pyramidal structure that supports the real bracing elements—cast parts in the form of shark fins, angel wings, biomorphic "silhouettes" or stabilizing blades—on which the desktop rests all the while giving the impression that it is floating. The Sarapis stool (1985), which owes its elementary metal profile to the severity and rusticity of its appearance, recalls—and the remark is not new—Picasso's "bicycle saddle-handlebars" (*Bull's Head*, 1942) or other Dadaist and surrealist images. With the Lola Mundo table and chair, whose metal legs adopt a graceful curve evocative of a ballerina's legs, technique is tinted with humor, and Starck's interest in pliable objects materializes.

But what really made Starck's success is the Juicy Salif lemon squeezer, which he designed for Alessi (1988). In spite of numerous critiques denouncing its shaky functionality, this object proved to be of major importance, insofar as it gave a vital impetus to a firm's strategy, in this case that of Alessi, who, for many years, had undertaken to offer a new generation of objects. It does not in fact concern objects to be used so much, but rather objects to give as presents, legitimized by the cultural aura surrounding the entire campaign (which began with Mendini's design of the Tea & Coffee Plaza collection) and by designers' names (Aldo Rossi for coffee makers, Michael Graves for kettles, etc.). This campaign came to a decisive turning point with Starck's lemon squeezer, and the success with which the Juicy Salif was blessed is inseparable from the photograph campaign then carried out for the advertisement. The lemon squeezer appears as a mysterious thing, a sort of drop lightly placed on three legs, a lunar vehicle with elongated shadows, a giant spider, an object come from elsewhere, an "alien." With Starck, Alessi succeeded in reinventing a mass market for a product whose market is largely saturated and in transforming a utilitarian object into a new type of decorative object and, at the end of the day, into a cult object.

Its success lies in the many levels of interpretation offered by a sign that is boldly stated yet enigmatic, and the complexity of elements contributing to its mysterious aspect. We are faced with an unsettling postmodern version of a "je ne sais quoi" sensation which eighteenth-century aesthetics saw as constituting a certain affinity with an object. An entire series of Starck's projects are presented as "alien" objects that are strange and disturbing figures but also strong, recognizable signs within the heterogeneous surroundings of urban or domestic life, and they are beyond ever being restored to order. From this viewpoint, the lemon squeezer is not just a useful object, for it also denotes another world, that of the pleasure of consumption.

Starck's work deserves much further analysis in terms of the interiors' elegance, the enigmatic side of the icon-objects, the connections spun between them, and other aspects. What seems compelling now, however, is to underscore how essential the presence of a unifying factor and of a communicable identity as a whole turns out to be, given the pragmatic or case by case manner in which Starck proceeds. Starck is searching for a strong, characterizing sign. Take the Tippy Jackson and Titos Apostos tables (1982), for example: open, they look like regular tables and their incisive style does not belie this normality in any way; folded up and hung on the wall, they appear as precise graphic signs, almost ideograms. These signs are certainly clearer in photographs and showrooms than in real life, as they are only explicit when the table is folded. But pursuing his quest, Starck has arrived at a series of variants. And so a family of signs, capable of living by themselves or applied to objects, is born. They are clear but ambiguous, rectilinear or curved, shaped like a horn or a flame: flower stem, feather or a splinter on a tree trunk, like in the W.W. stool (1990). As for the droplet form, mentioned previously with regard to the lemon squeezer and which is a leitmotif in American design of the 1930s, it haunts a great many objects. Lamps, vases, knives and other utensils thus become disturbing recognizable visual signs, a sort of Starck signature, brand or logo. This sign appears almost everywhere, including on the Royalton beds, in the form of tiny vases, and even on the Motó 6.5 (Aprilia), where it is only revealed by the form of someone sitting on back of the seat, when seen from behind. Endowed with signs of this kind, these objects tend to be identified as belonging much more to the all-embracing Starck/star "designer label" than to a style or a firm. Thus Starck's design work becomes sign production—a production that aims, in a pragmatic way, to define the visibility of an object case by case. And, in this sense, it also becomes an instrument of differentiation, an asset in what is called the "new marketing era."

In offering recurrent signals and symptomatic traits that openly belong to a defined personal language, Starck is miles away from those stylistic attempts and proposals for systems of forms and decoration that made the heyday of Italian postmodern design. Apparently, only Paolo Deganello, whose organic forms melt into an inorganic and programmatic play on the opposition of lines and materials, could hold his attention.

It should be added that Starck finds a second unifying factor in the names he gives his objects. Often, they come from the characters in the novels of Philip K. Dick, the great visionary science-fiction writer, guru of the "cybergeneration" and author of, among others, *Do Androids Dream of Electric Sheep?* on which Ridley Scott based his brilliant movie *Blade Runner*. Starck's composite world, where races and forms are mixed and nothing is really what it appears to be, seems to have become a metaphor for his idea of postmodernity, which allows him to bear witness to his time.

Very attentive to the building of his own myth, Starck set up a sort of collaboration with the "design-oriented" firms most concerned by communications strategies and the evolution of advertising. Thus, for the first time, the designer's image overshadows the product. The Miss Sissi ad (1991) is a perfect example: shot from below, Starck's huge silhouette is like a Gargantua towering over tiny lamps (it recalls, in passing, the French-born designer Raymond Loewy, who habitually had himself photographed in front of the locomotives and ships that he had "streamlined"). Many of Flos' other advertisements are consistent with these characteristics, notably the ad for the Rosy Angelis lamp (1994), which was presented at the same time as the reedition of the Luminator floor lamp by Achille Castiglioni (an Italian designer who is a kindred spirit for Starck, undoubtedly because of his anti-intellectualism, his irony and his pragmatic, anti-ideological way of working). Starck has also transformed himself into an offhanded juggler, balancing the Dr. Glob chair (1985) on one finger, or a resigned peddler suspended from a hook (for Alessi) with other cooking utensils. In Italy, architect-designers had customarily practiced a very reserved kind of narcissism, by appearing in photographs (often done by renowned photographers) reproduced in magazines; but they almost never featured themselves in advertisements. The firms for which Starck works have consecrated him as the representative of a new star system, that of design, which wants to resemble that of cinema, fashion and, perhaps above all, rock music; design has thus made its definitive entry into communications society. And Starck seems to deliver himself up to a body art sort of experience, in which the designer's body is the medium—a representation of the change that has occurred simultaneously in the designer's image and in the status of design.

At the same time, the importance of communications strategies for firms has evolved. Often entrusted to fashion photographers, catalogues and advertisements aspire to offer much more than a lifestyle: a world carrying values, a "mindstyle," sometimes going to the point of trying to become actual magazines, as Benetton did with *Color*. Incidentally, it is no accident that for the cover of its first issue (January 1996) of the magazine-catalogue *ED,* Driade chose a picture of Starck with empty eyes, a satanic character emblematic of the alien or of a horror film.

Over the course of the Italian period that concerns us, a profile of a professional very different from the typical Italian architect-designer emerged around 1985–1995. This new figure belongs precisely to Starck/design star. A new figure, yes, but one who does not necessarily ask to be imitated: rather, Starck promotes a sort of legitimatization of every possible type of choice, both on a professional level and regarding the project—and that can be seen in young designers today.

From another point of view, numerous Italian firms also changed their way of understanding and communicating during this same period. If, in the 1980s, they called on postmodern architects to bolster the appeal of their own image on an international scale, today, they produce projects by talented young designers from around the world, thus becoming a sort of laboratory for international design. Moreover, during the past few years, methods have changed with the expansion of globalization: making good products and making them known no longer suffices; the message to promote these days is a particular "ambiance" and a global project through the "spectacularization" of a firm's image.

Clearly, Starck is not the only one who made the strategies of Italian firms evolve and, likewise, his career does not owe everything to those companies. But it is certain that the two were interlinked and had an undeniable impact on each other—one powerful enough to constitute an actual era in design. This demonstrates the entrepreneurial intelligence and open-mindedness of the Italian firms, as well as Starck's conceptual power.

Translated by Elizabeth Jian-Xing Too

Stéphane Laurent

Time Traveler

The Work and Stance of Philippe Starck in the Perspective of Design Heritage

Countless books and articles have come out during the lifetime of today's most famous designer, Philippe Starck. Some track his latest creations while others attempt to analyze the reasons for his success; still others focus on his personal philosophy. However, and probably because the history of design and technology is granted little importance—is it paradoxical to speak of history regarding an object of consumption subjected to factuality and obsolescence?—few writings have tried to examine the work and stance of Philippe Starck in the perspective of design heritage.

STARCK VIS-À-VIS LOEWY

Jane Withers has compared Philippe Starck to Raymond Loewy.[1] It is true that their careers present many similarities: both are of mixed origins and, by a strange coincidence, of Alsatian descent from their fathers' side of the family and Auvergnian from their mothers' side; very talented draftsmen, both have a substantial and comprehensive body of work despite the fact that they are autodidacts, they enjoy extensive international recognition, move in jet-setting circles, and have an innate sense of the media and their roles in design.

Clearly, though, the evolution of thought and Western mentalities widens the generation gap: while Loewy, a former 1914-18 *poilu*, is a sort of golden boy brought forth by the American miracle, who contributed to launching the profession of industrial design consultant, Starck, also from a bourgeois background, is a rebel child who remained true to France. Far from the self-made man who plays up exception, his is a modest triumph as he is part and parcel of his time. He was nineteen in May 1968 and, although he says he saw nothing of the events during his brief stay at the "preppy" Ecole Camondo, the notion of freedom of speech specific to that period has left its mark on him.

For Starck and Loewy, graphic arts is an essential tool of the design process and an irreplaceable language of communication. Loewy began his artistic career as a fashion and magazine illustrator, became a master in rendering, and executed a considerable number of roughs, whereas Starck makes reams of sketches, which form the groundwork of his projects. Their completion and realization are entrusted to his collaborators.

They both live the high life with residences on several continents, but Starck is protective of his private life. He is a fan of rock and roll and science fiction (many of his works' titles were inspired by Philip K. Dick), prefers motorcycles to big American cars, and never poses in a suit and tie or with an impeccable hairdo. Instead, he rags the viewer with his prizewinning self-derision. The American myth lauded by his father leaves him perplexed. He undoubtedly gets a good laugh out of 1930s Flash Gordon-inspired streamline as well as photographs of Loewy posing as an astronaut when the agency he co-directed with Snaith worked for NASA. However, they might also be surprisingly familiar since, as a child, Philippe woke up every day across from his father's office, which was filled with ground-breaking aircraft plans and sophisticated materials. “My father was completely bio-ionic,” he explains. “He had a plastic nose, all his teeth were false, and after having messed up on a landing, he had a bolt sticking out of his arm.”[2] Though Starck Sr. seems more immoderate than the American designer, the latter could well have followed in his footsteps: “At the age of ten, he saw the Brazilian inventor Santos Dumont fly one hundred meters over the Bois de Boulogne in a handmade airplane. Filling his sketchbooks with drawings of automobiles and locomotives, he invented a ‘toy’ for himself at the age of fifteen—a small plane propelled by a motor with an elastic, which won him the illustrious James Gordon Bennett Cup. The most significant thing in this story is that, already, the youthful designer instantly thought of having his model plane patented and sold under the name Ayrel.”[3] Can we construe this virtuosity in design as a matter of impetuousness, firsthand technical experimentation, and patenting? By the close ties they each maintained with the field of invention, both Starck and Loewy tend to confirm this hypothesis.

Could there be other contributing factors, more personal and profound? In a famous essay,[4] Erwin Panofsky uncovered the importance of melancholy in artistic production. This phenomenon has never been analyzed in connection with the key figures of the applied arts. Starck and Loewy have both lived turbulent personal lives, marked by divorce and death. Philippe Starck, who stopped seeing his father at the age of ten, lived a strange life with his mother. Without having spoken to him since he had stopped seeing him, Starck lost his father when he was about thirty years old. As for Loewy's parents, they died suddenly, probably of the Spanish flu, at a time when the young man had just arrived in the United States and did not yet have any real professional future. In 1945, he divorced Jean Thomson after fourteen years of marriage and married, in 1948, Viola Erickson, who was much younger than he was and whose beauty accompanied him in numerous photo sessions. Given his insatiable thirst for success and representativeness and his overindulgence in self-promotion, it could be asked if these excesses as a whole conceal a kind of buried hopelessness. To what degree do they weigh upon his work? That has been deemed the realm of the unsaid and never disclosed, perhaps out of fear of the sturdily built edifice collapsing.

When faced with the inevitable obsolescence of the image, of mentalities and even of the manufactured object, the design work of Raymond Loewy—who could have been a grandfather to Starck, and who was finishing his career in France when the latter was just starting—suddenly "ages"; all the more so as the diligence Loewy puts into serving the capitalist system is ridiculed by the alternative social design to which Starck lends a resolutely political direction today. It would be a mistake, however, to assume that the "old" master would have disowned the "young" master. The entire profession, including Loewy's spiritual progeny—his old collaborators in particular—acknowledges the new prodigy's talent.

STARCK AND HIS PREDECESSORS

Other days, other ways, it would seem? The design process created by Philippe Starck is in fact rooted in the past. Starck is a figure whose multiple facets harmonize with those of his predecessors in a sort of synthetic brilliance.

One of the most significant aspects of Starck's design is that it is founded on a discourse. And the discourse of a designer cannot be disassociated from his or her function.[5] An auxiliary actor of industrial society since the nineteenth century, the designer can only make himself indispensable within the cog wheels of production as long as the importance of aesthetic added value as offered by an artist to the enterprise can be justified by an augmentation of sales. For long, many entrepreneurs have remained, and still remain today, reticent toward the idea of investing in design. For them, the designer appeared to be a troublemaker, a stance that Starck knew exactly how to exploit to his advantage. As a general rule, they resort to the designer's skills, less for philanthropic or aesthetic reasons than for the profit they can make from it.

It was mainly the American designers of the interwar period who succeeded in convincing the business world that the economy's modernization could also be achieved through design. In order to do this, they employed a very pragmatic professional discourse. To the contrary, the De Stijl movement, the Bauhaus school and constructivism, which were artistic avant-gardes sometimes in spite of their complicity with the echelons of power, played a marginal role that was often anti-establishment and always experimental and remonstrative, and their finished works were supported by theories. In a way, Starck is located in the postindustrial sphere of influence since he reaps the fruits of positivist conviction, while bypassing them with a discourse that goes back to the avant-garde. Does he not thank Ettore Sottsass for having "relaxed" the atmosphere of functionalism? Besides, there would be much to say on the tie he maintains with postmodern thinking, as well as on the playful, dreamlike character of his comments and objects.

But for all that, the content of his discourse is not entirely new. Thus, when he insists on the necessity of conceiving "honest" objects that would contribute to restoring love or, in other words, that would be factors of social harmony,

Starck makes reference to a concept developed by nineteenth-century industrial artists and their defenders, such as Count de Laborde in France and William Morris in England.[6] In a lecture published in 1878, "The Lesser Arts of Life," the latter explains that "the decorative arts pursue a dual objective: to make the people take pleasure in *using* the things they have to use and to find as much pleasure in *making* the objects they are obliged to make." He adds: "We will then be able to enhance our lives with the pleasure of *buying* merchandise at a fair price; as well as the pleasure of *selling* merchandise whose high quality, in relation to its price and labor, will be our pride and joy."[7] Clearly, however, Morris, who was known for his humanist and socialist positions, goes further than Starck insofar as he immediately affirms a vertical political structure that includes a reform of all human activities related to the object. Moreover, with Good Goods, which was commissioned by La Redoute, the French designer belatedly became aware of the appeal of investing mail-order catalogues, which, as the Manufrance catalogue attests, have been vehicles for disseminating taste to homes since the nineteenth century.

A PERENNIAL NOVELTY

Starck undoubtedly owes his longevity to a balance between magic and classicism. He says he rejects trends to make an object last longer, but fashion nonetheless ends up catching hold of it. He may well be curled up in his creative bubble, but the fact remains that this bubble is porous to details and to undefined fields grasping his attention. Starck works in a "haute couture" way, using an unfailing, reduced workforce, in the spirit of an old-fashioned atelier. Like Dürer and Gallé, who possess the dual skills of entrepreneur and artist, he conducts business and his work simultaneously. He is classical in his search for essence and purity—two virtues of antique art—yet his objects are treated like archaic figures. Is it a legacy from the 1980s? In any case, they gain a magic universality characteristic of that epoch.

Starck's evolution led him to abolish the divide between the decorative arts and design, proving that the latter was born out of the former and that opposing them is an outmoded debate. In this, he follows the course of Peter Behrens who, at the beginning of the twentieth century, went from Art Nouveau to reaching the industry. Starck began as an interior architect who presented an inflatable house at the Salon de l'Enfance (1967) and designed furniture and fittings for Pierre Cardin and Quasar. The renewal of President Mitterrand's apartments at the Palais de l'Elysée was also undertaken in his capacity as an interior designer. Starting in the late 1980s, he entered on a shift by co-signing architectural plans and designing objects like televisions, motorbikes and electric appliances that featured an ornateness and a theatricality particular to the decorative.

Starck offers a name, a signature worth its commercial weight. An object designed by Starck has value in terms of status and price. In 1986, he modestly said to a journalist that he had ninety-seven projects underway. But how many of them were completed? Numerous candidates were put on the shelf, often because they did not accept his conditions. This freedom of choice and refusal, which belongs only to the "great and illustrious," allows him to pay no heed to the traditional means of communication necessary to the promotion of a design agency.

No designer has ever had so much power. Loewy never had a completely stable position, even at the pinnacle of his glory. Known for his extravagance, he was forced to have an associate in order to ensure the survival of his New York agency. His agency in Paris, the Compagnie de l'Esthétique Industrielle, was only able to balance its budget by its graphic design activity. After all is said and done, if we want to find Starck a predecessor as wooed as he, or perhaps even more, on account of a commission from the Prince, it would be suitable to go to the field of painting: Nicolas Poussin, destined for Louis XIII's court through his patron Fréart de Chantelou; Bernini, summoned by Louis XIV; or Leonardo da Vinci himself, whom Francis I brought to France after the Italian Wars, and who had already lent his multifaceted genius to other sovereigns of the peninsula, including the Medicis in Florence and the Sforzas in Milan. Closer to our time, Picasso naturally comes to mind. His relationship to power held more of a political engagement, but the irony is that his descendants were to confer the use of his name to a car. Nevertheless, by virtue of the omnipresence of drawing, which must respond to the unbridled cadence of the projecting imagination, and by virtue of the importance of conception over realization, it would certainly be more appropriate to link Starck's inventiveness to the line of artist-engineers that goes from Leonardo da Vinci to Jean Prouvé.

Inscribed in a democratic process and in one of globalization, Starck swaps elitist commissions for mass consumption and, no longer satisfied with the European market, he roams the world of contractors. This performance is a success because he has transformed his status as a designer into that of a rock star. He confessed in 1985: "I am not a designer, I am more of a show-biz artiste. Like them, I am paid before the concert. I do not have contracts. I do not have a plan for execution. Either people want it or not."[8] It is indeed an original revamping of the profession's status!

The erosion of Starck's designs in the face of time remains an unresolved question. For now, it is important to situate this major figure of contemporary design as an heir not always acknowledged as such.

Translated by Elizabeth Jian-Xing Too

1. See *Raymond Loewy, un pionnier du design américain*, ex. cat. June 27-September 24, 1990, (Paris: Centre Pompidou, 1990). / See *Raymond Loewy: Pioneer of American Industrial Design*, ed. Angela Schönberger, trans. Ian Robson and Eileen Martin. (New York: Munich Prestel, 1990).
2. From an interview, in Christine Colin, *Starck* (Paris: Mardaga, 1988), p. 19.
3. Evert Endt, "Paris-New York. Les débuts de Raymond Loewy," *Raymond Loewy, un pionnier du design américain, op. cit.*, p. 24. / Evert Endt, "The Early Years of Raymond Loewy," *Raymond Loewy: Pioneer of American Industrial Design*, op. cit., p. 24.
4. Klibansky Raymond, Panofsky Erwin, Saxl Fritz, *Saturn and Melancholy: Studies in the History of Natural Philosophy, Religion, and Art* [1923] (New York: Basic Books, 1964).
5. Stéphane Laurent, *Chronologie du design* (Paris: Flammarion, 1999).
6. The success of objets d'art at World's Fairs leads to a reflection on their role in social progress. In France, Count de Laborde and, in England, William Morris made them into visionary commentators and critics. In particular, they proposed daring reforms announcing the upheaval of the decorative arts that was to produce Art Nouveau. See Stéphane Laurent, *Les Arts appliqués en France, genèse d'un enseignement* (Paris, CHTS, 1999).
7. William Morris, *Contre l'art d'élite*, (Paris: Hermann, 1985), p. 28.
8. In an interview with Christine Colin, *Starck*, op. cit., p. 20.

Christopher Mount

French Kissing in the U.S.A.

Starck in America

The French Revolution, and the American Revolution that preceded it, are monumental historical events that are uniquely intertwined. The founding fathers of the United States borrowed many of the concepts of the inalienable rights of man from the treatises of the great French philosopher Jean-Jacques Rousseau. The result was the shifting of the original emphasis of the Bill of Rights, from a document favoring the rights of only property holders to one that emphasized the rights of all men. In a far less prodigious moment, America has once again looked to France to find guidance in the democratization of a part of our culture. Philippe Starck's work in America—his furniture, objects and hotels—has been a major catalyst in the recent blossoming of interest in the field of design among the general public. He has helped popularize what was once an arcane subject. Along the way, he also has sold countless thousands of objects and even created a celebrity status for himself in America.

He has achieved this, at least partially, by force of personality, but most significantly through his work, particularly his small affordable products, like his Dr. Cheese toothbrush, the ubiquitous Juicy Salif lemon squeezer and his chic hotels decorated on behalf of the developer Ian Schrager. His popularity has coincided with a period when America's economy is relatively robust and the public is eagerly ready for something new. The majority of Starck's American consumers have grown up viewing substantial amounts of television and seem to share an acute visual sophistication that previous generations don't possess. Starck addresses the current American spirit: "My goal in this democratization of design is to make possible the most joyful and exciting things and experiences for the maximum number of people. Today, we don't need more design, more pretensions—we need more happiness and more magic available to everyone."

Unfortunately, Starck and his democratizing tendencies often have been misunderstood and frequently dismissed by critics because they are contrary to the ideas and canons of the modernist movement of the last century. These earlier concepts have become so ingrained in the way we look at objects that Starck's work hasn't always been accepted and is often misinterpreted. In the late nineteenth century, the call for the democratization of design began with William Morris and his plea for "art for everyone." Twentieth-century European movements that followed fought for beautiful, functional and, most importantly, affordable design for all. This philosophy was born in the aftermath of the devastation of World War I. Figures like Alvar Aalto, Marcel Breuer and Gerrit Rietveld hoped to rebuild Europe in an orderly manner, creating a new harmony based on the rationalism of the machine.

Stylistically, they had taken to heart Adolf Loos' belief that "ornament was a crime" and had delighted in the use of new austere forms in which the Platonic shapes of the machine were the model. For the traditional European modernist, the finished product, whether it was a bowl or appliance or piece of furniture, must be relatively simple in appearance without decoration and sensitive to the needs of its purchaser. Functionalism and practicality were paramount concerns. The modernist designer strove for a timelessness quality, expressed in form. This was essential, since it prevented quick obsolescence

and ignored the whims of fashion. All of these beliefs were part of the fundamental search for the absolute and the non-subjective in design.
Today, despite the fact that Europe has long ago rebuilt from the devastation of World War I and World War II, and that the United States has developed into an economic superpower, many still judge design by these somewhat antiquated ideas and conditions. Should we still choose to value design by the merits that were established while Europe was rehabilitating or America was a young nation finding its way? Perhaps Western democracies and their relatively wealthy economies don't need objects that respond so severely to the issues of practicality and functionalism as they once did. This seems to be the essential question Starck is asking with his large body of work. Maybe the contemporary consumer needs something else that isn't necessarily the prototype of "good design." Starck has other priorities, more current ones that better address what today's public wants. Perhaps the best example of this is his intentionally silly and superfluous Gnome side tables, which hold just "snacks and refreshments" and snicker along with the designer at the modernist canon of functionalism.
Historically, the rigid laws of modernism were never embraced in France or the United States as they were in parts of northern Europe. Subsequently, the leftist tendencies at the core of much of architecture and industrial or graphic design were ignored by the French and Americans. Starck's primarily apolitical work fits more comfortably into the zeitgeist of both America and France, as well as the consumer culture of many Asian nations. For Starck, rationalism and the desire for timelessness are unnecessary and outdated ideals. Instead, like some sort of design utilitarian (in the spirit of John Stuart Mill), Starck wants to evoke happiness! The kind of happiness that for him cannot be achieved solely through

the clean serious lines of modernism. As he recently stated in an interview with *The New York Times*, "I want to help people have a better life." However, he is not speaking of the sort of contentment found in a simple well-made object, or say a piece of Aalto furniture, but instead of the kind of emotional delight created by his whimsical and often overtly decorative products.

In many respects, Starck has subverted the traditional relationship between product and consumer quite shrewdly by developing and encouraging an almost irrational desire for his quirky objects. His products are the objects of longing, not utility. They create what is analogous to the well-worn literary theme of a hero or heroine falling victim to a yearning that they consciously know will only lead to ruinous consequences. Starck has transformed many Americans into design-loving Humbert Humberts or Madame Bovarys, whose passions are unfettered by reasoning. We want his things, but don't really know why. Starck makes little that is necessary; however, he seems to give the public what they want, even before they know it. It is, in some sense, the most American of principles, a concept that has helped build our enormous consumer culture: first make something and then create a market for it.

Starck has been extremely clever in his infiltration of the American market by starting small, with inexpensive products that don't require much of a commitment from the consumer. One of his great skills as a designer is to transform the most ordinary object and infuse it with a uniqueness, resulting in the consumer's desire for it. This is the primary reason why Starck is so successful, particularly from the manufacturers' point of view, because they know that his imprint can transform the most mundane into a popular seller. Objects like the Juicy Salif lemon squeezer, Dr. Skud flyswatter, Excalibur toilet brush and the Miss Sissi lamp are all things that function as both useful objects and as decorative home elements that can be displayed like sculpture. As Starck himself has admitted about the Juicy Salif, “This is not a very good lemon squeezer, but that’s not its only function. I had this idea that when a couple gets married it’s the sort of thing they would get as a wedding present.” It is a home accessory intended to amuse and entertain and add a visual element to counterbalance the more serious parts of the home.

As his popularity has grown in America, because of the success of both his hotel interiors and these small, charming and relatively inexpensive products, he has also recently experienced success in the larger American furniture market. His La Marie, Dr. No, Miss Coco and the recently introduced Ero-s Chairs have all shared a large popularity and a unique place in the market. Part of the impetus for their success is their flexibility; made of plastic—and in a few instances with some metal—they can function outside as well as inside. The wonderful Miss Coco conveniently collapses and is the perfect chair for crowded urban apartment dwellers, who might like to invite more than six to dinner. These pieces of furniture are much admired by Americans for their price, ranging from around $150 to $370 for the more expensive Ero-s. The chairs allow the young family just starting out or the poor college student to add some style into what might otherwise be a drab interior. In 2000, Emeco, an American manufacturer of one of the country’s few vernacular pieces of furniture, the 304 chair (produced in 1944 for the military), asked Starck to update the chair. Starck made only small adjustments to the series, adding a rocker version, wisely deciding not to completely redesign the classic, but instead subtly improving and updating the concept.

If in reworking the Emeco chair, Starck worked with a truly classic American design, then for his recent series of objects for Target, Starck has chosen one of the United States’ largest and most innovative retailers. Introduced in the spring of 2002 at the Milan Furniture Fair, the first selection of products includes a variety of relatively serious useful objects, such as a magazine rack, letter sorter, tape dispenser, curling set and electronic toothbrush for adults. But perhaps the most interesting part of the introductory pieces is the series of items for children and infants. As American culture has overwhelmed Europe, Starck hopes to introduce his sense of style to the very young of America and perhaps, in turn, reverse some of the cultural trade deficit created by the overwhelming influence of American popular culture on European youth. The objects for children include a pop-up playhouse, baby bottle, toy car, baby monitor, spill-proof cup and toilet training set. All of the designs exude a sort of exuberance and sense of fun that Starck products—even for adults—frequently possess. Here, the spirit has found its perfect manifestation. The baby monitor and spill-proof bottle are particularly smart and satisfying, in that they introduce a humorous and faux sense of luxury to two of the drabbest utilitarian objects. The baby monitor has a fake encrusted jewel embedded in a metal casing, so that mothers can wear it without feeling dowdy, and the cup's plastic is etched as if to suggest Waterford crystal for baby. Starck has avoided the usual ordinariness of infant things; this is further evident with the toys for older children, a stylish toy car and a wonderfully architectural tent-like playhouse. The tent, with its vibrant color and pleasing abstract shape, may do for American children what his innovative hotels have done for their parents.

Although Starck has achieved a phenomenal degree of success as a result of his products and furniture in the United States, perhaps his most popular and comprehensive success in terms of democratizing design has come in the form of his interiors, particularly his hotels. His American hotels include the Royalton, Paramount and Hudson in New York, the Hotel Delano in Miami, the Mondrian in Los Angeles and the recently completed Clift in San Francisco. It is with the hotels that Starck's penchant for showmanship is most evident. In the spirit of the great American Barnum Bailey, Starck's hotels are filled with surprise, wit and a tasteful tendency toward exaggeration. As Starck is quoted in Conway Lloyd Morgan's book, *Starck:* "Being away from home is disorienting for hotel guests, but after settling them down, we want to give them pleasure with mental and visual jokes. If people look closely, they can discover the secret life and relationship between objects." Perhaps this is best represented in the green apples (contrasted with the austere white interior) waiting outside each door at the Delano. He has introduced a sense of theater into the hotel business that was sadly lacking in America and created, particularly in Miami and New York, spaces which even those who are not registered come to see. These are new kinds of public spaces—not just like a restaurant, café, nightclub or bar, but instead places where you can gawk and soak in a certain implied glamor from the surroundings.

Starck and his client for the hotels, Ian Schrager, seem to have hit on a successful and certainly profitable recipe. Once again, like his other designs, Starck's hotels are not all at the luxury price point. In fact, the Paramount and Hudson—by New York standards—are affordable, particularly when one takes into account the additional appeal of the stylish interiors. The designer is acutely aware of the fact that the experience of going to a successful hotel must be significantly different from simply staying at home or staying at another place. These interiors are about drama, and this begins at the door: the flowing white curtains on the porch of the Delano, the green glowing escalator that whisks you to the reception desk at the Hudson or the long purple carpet that leads the visitor down the lobby of the Royalton, for example. All these welcoming elements suggest the beginnings of a theatrical experience. In other parts, a sense of drama is enhanced by severe juxtapositions of scale: the large potted plants at the Mondrian or the enormous Vermeer reproductions in the rooms of the Paramount. These interiors, and particularly the guestrooms, can be homey, as a hotel often is, yet also foreign and sometimes unnerving at the same time. The white sanatorium-like rooms of the Delano in Miami are the perfect example, but as Starck would ask, why spend money to stay at a place that feels just like home?

Certainly another reason for the success of the Schrager and Starck hotels is their evocation of romance. There is an inherent sexiness to Starck's designs that seems to particularly intrigue the more puritanical nature of Americans. Whether frequently acknowledged or not, hotels are sexy places, for newlyweds on a honeymoon, the married couple on an intimate getaway, the clandestine meeting or for even inspiring the business executive's fantasies. Starck is keenly aware of this and his hotels feature lots of blush coaches for cuddling, dark corners for couples to share and rooms that are frequently so intimate that the bed is the most comfortable place to sit and communicate. There is much that is subversive and hidden about his interiors; his furnishings and interiors intentionally transport guests from their mundane existence to another place, liberating them from everyday problems and worries. What could be more conducive to romance? There is an implied comfort to the over-stuffed couches that line many of his lobbies, but perhaps the most overtly romantic places are his poolside areas at the Mondrian and the bed-like couches at the Delano, with curtains that close shut for privacy.

In the end, Americans have embraced Starck's designs for many of the same reasons why we have been attracted to much of French culture. A Frenchman might argue that it is simply a question of quality, and that may be. But the answer goes deeper. There is an unattainable sense of extravagance to his products and hotels, even if the actual cost is frequently not extravagant at all. Everyone likes things that seem a bit bad for us, and Americans have long craved the rich foods, romantic films, decorative furniture and impractical haute couture produced in France. We have looked across the Atlantic frequently to relieve us from our rather puritanical and staid selves. As a young country with little cultural history of our own, we are attracted to the self-confidence and the theatrical elements of Starck's work. He is a savvy businessman and designer who has brought a certain decadence to the American home and the experience of a hotel, all at an affordable price, and we have welcomed this with open arms.

Published to coincide with the exhibition *Philippe Starck,* presented
at the Centre Pompidou, Musée National d'Art Moderne/Centre de Création Industrielle
from February 26 to May 12, 2003, this book was conceived and edited by:

Valérie Guillaume

Curator at the Musée National d'Art Moderne/Centre de Création Industrielle,
Department of Design. Author of many publications on material culture, fashion and design.

THE AUTHORS

Christine Colin

A representative of the Délégation aux Arts Plastiques, in charge of the Fonds National d'Art Contemporain design collection. Curator of the exhibition *Moins et Plus* at the Musée d'Art Moderne de Saint-Étienne Métropole, 2002. Author of many books and articles on Philippe Starck.

Benoît Heilbrunn

Ph.D. in management science, Université de Paris-Dauphine, teaches marketing, communications and design at the École de Management de Lyon (EM Lyon). His latest book, *Le Logo,* was published by PUF in 2001.

Stéphane Laurent

Holder of the *agrégation,* associate professor in the History of Art and Industry department at Université de Paris I Panthéon-Sorbonne. Author of many books on the history of design, including *Chronologie du design,* which was published by Flammarion in 1999.

Christopher Mount

Design historian, teaches in New York at the Parsons School of Design and in the Masters Program for Decorative Arts at the Cooper-Hewitt Museum. Formerly a curator in the Department of Architecture and Design at the Museum of Modern Art, and the editor in chief of *I.D. Magazine.*

Michel Onfray

Doctor of Philosophy and founder, in 2002, of the Université Populaire in Caen. He has published over twenty books in which he puts forward a theory of hedonism.

Vanni Pasca

Architect, design consultant. Teaches design history and theory at Politecnico di Milano and coordinates the industrial design Ph.D. program in the architecture faculty at Palermo University. Curator of many exhibitions. His book, *Vico Magistretti,* was published by Electa in 2000.

Sophie Trelcat

Architect, teacher and writer for the magazine *L'Architecture d'Aujourd'hui,* she has published many articles on contemporary architecture.

Bibliography

MONOGRAPHS AND GENERAL WORKS

2001

Bauer, Christine, *Le Cas Philippe Starck ou de la construction de la notoriété*, Paris, L'Harmattan, "Communication" series.

La Collection design du Centre Georges Pompidou, Paris, Jousset, Marie-Laure (dir.), Éditions du Centre Pompidou.

Colin, Christine, "Philippe Starck signe *Magic Slabe* et *Cicatrices de Lux*, deux produits significatifs de la nouvelle politique de gamme de Flos. Qu'en dit-il ?", in Christine Colin (dir.), *Design et Gammes*, Paris, Industries françaises de l'ameublement/ Les Villages/Hazan, pp. 100-102.

2000

La Collection architecture du Centre Georges Pompidou, Guiheux, Alain (dir.), Paris, Éditions du Centre Pompidou.

Colin, Christine, "Bonne marchandise (Good Goods ou l'utopie et 8 T-shirts)", in *Design et utopies*., Paris, Industries françaises de l'ameublement/Les Villages/ Hazan, pp. 8-21.

Ibid., "Les produits de rêve," interview with Elsa Francès, pp. 32-37.

Starck, Philippi, Simone (dir.), Cologne/London/Paris, Taschen.

1999

Carmel-Arthur, Judith, *Philippe Starck*, London, Carlton.

Morgan, Conway Lloyd, *Philippe Starck*, Paris, Adam Biro.

Sweet, Fay, *Philippe Starck. Subverchic Design*, London, Thames and Hudson.

1998

Alessi, Alberto, *L'Usine à rêves. Alessi depuis 1921*, Cologne, Könemann.

1997

Mello, Patrizia, *Progetti in movimento Philippe Starck*, Florence, Edizioni Festina Lente.

1996

Dictionnaire international des arts appliqués et du design, Barré-Despond, Arlette (dir.), Paris, Éditions du Regard.

"Extraits de conversation de Philippe Starck avec Sophie Tasma-Anargyros et Pierre Doze," in *Starck*, Simone Philippi (dir.), Cologne/London/Paris, Taschen.

Martin, Marijke, Wagenaar, Cor, Welkamp, Annette, *Alessandro & Francesco Mendini, Philippe Starck, Michele De Lucchi, Coop Himmelb(l)au in Groningen*, Groningen, Groninger Museum.

Philippe Starck: distordre. Dialogue sur le design entre Alberto Alessi et Philippe Starck, Meneguzzo, Marco (dir.), Milan, Electa/Alessi.

1995

Cent chefs-d'œuvre de la collection du Vitra Design Museum, Vegesack, Alexander von (dir.), Weil am Rhein, Vitra Design Museum.

"Ubiquité, sélection de la contradiction," (interview with Philippe Starck by Christine Colin and Jean-Bernard Magescas), in *Fonction et Fiction.* Liège, Industries françaises de l'ameublement/ Les Villages/Mardaga, pp. 8-15.

1994

Bertoni, Franco, *The Architecture of Philippe Starck,* London, Academy Editions.

Id., *Philippe Starck. L'Architecture,* Liège, Margada.

Colin, Christine, "Le tout authentique," in *Autentik,* Liège, Industries françaises de l'ameublement/Les Villages in Mardaga, pp. 58-75.

1993

Fillion, Odile, "Philippe Starck, le juste produit," in *Modernité et Modestie,* Liège, Industries françaises de l'ameublement/ Les Villages in Mardaga, pp. 50-63.

1992

Hideo, Saitoh, Stroeter, João Rodolfo, *Interior Design in Cafes and Restaurants,* Tokyo, Bijutsu Schuppan-Sia.

Irace, Fulvio, *Dimore metropolitane. Cafe, ristoranti, alberghi di Philippe Starck. Proposti da Driade,* Milan, Electa.

1991

Boissière, Olivier, *Philippe Starck,* Cologne, Taschen.

1990

Nouveau théâtre de Tokyo, Japon. Jean Nouvel et associés, Philippe Starck, Tonka, Hubert (dir.), Paris, Éditions du Demi-Cercle, "Architecture & Cie, États & lieux" series, 1990.

1988

Colin, Christine, *Design aujourd'hui,* Paris, Flammarion.

Id., *Starck,* Liège, Pierre Mardaga.

1987

Renaud, Philippe, *Philippe Starck. Mobilier 1970-1987,* Marseille, Michel Aveline.

EXHIBITION CATALOGUES

2000

La Donation Kartell. Un environnement plastique 1949-1999, Jousset, Marie-Laure (dir.), Paris, Éditions du Centre Pompidou.

1995

13 nach Memphis Design zwischen Askese und Sinnlichkeit, Frankfurt, Museum für Kunsthandwerk.

Machado, Rodolfo, El-Khoury, Rodolphe, *Monolithic Architecture,* Pittsburgh, Carnegie Museum of Art, 1995-1996, Munich/New York, Prestel.

1993

Is Starck a Designer?, London, Design Museum.

1991

Formes des métropoles. Nouveaux designs en Europe, Paris, Éditions du Centre Pompidou, "Inventaires" series.

1990

Les Années VIA, exhibition cat. (Musée des arts décoratifs, april 24-aug 26 1990), Paris, Union des arts décoratifs.

L'Art de Vivre. Decorative Arts and Design in France (1789-1989), New York, Cooper-Hewitt Museum, March 30 to Aug. 6, 1989, London, Thames and Hudson.

Jean Nouvel, Christian de Portzamparc, Philippe Starck, XLVIe Venise Biennal, Pavillon français, may 27-sept. 30 1990, Rome, Carte Segrete.

1988

Les Années 50, Paris, Éditions du Centre Pompidou.

Le Design français. 1960-1990, Paris, Éditions du Centre Pompidou.

Design Heute, Massstäbe. Formgebung zwischen Industrie und Kunst-Stück, Frankfurt, Deutsches Architekturmuseum.

1987

Les Cent Chaises 1887-1987, Boulogne-Billancourt, Centre culturel.

Nouvelles tendances. Les avant-gardes de la fin du xxe siècle, Paris, Éditions du Centre Pompidou.

1986

Intérieur 86, 10e Biennale internationale de la créativité dans l'habitat, Courtrai (Belgium), Intérieur.

1985

Art et Industrie, Paris, Musée national des monuments français.

Contemporary Landscape from the Horizon of Postmodern Design, exhibition cat., Kyoto, National Museum of Art.

Nouveaux plaisirs d'architecture, Paris, Éditions du Centre Pompidou.

NEWSPAPERS, JOURNALS (SELECTION OF ARTICLES)

Abitare

Malfatti, Patrizia, "Nuovo paradigma" (St. Martins Lane Hotel, London), n° 391, Jan. 2000, pp. 158-164.

AD, Architectural Digest

Trocme, Suzanne, "Hôtel à Londres, la clé des songes" (Sanderson Hotel, London), n° 7, Nov. 2000, pp. 106-117.

Architectural Record

Stephens, Suzanne, "Philippe Starck's Colorfest in a London Hotel" (St. Martins Lane Hotel, London), vol. 188, n° 1, Jan. 2000, pp. 90-95.

Stein, Karen D., "Rags to Riches. The Royalton Hotel New York. Designers: Philippe Starck, Gruzen Samton Steinglass Architects," vol. 177, n° 3, March 1989, pp. 94-99.

Id., "Buildings Types Study. The World According to Starck" (Manin restaurant, Tokyo), vol. 175, n° 11, Sept. 1987, pp. 102-106.

Id., "Buildings Types Study 632. Record Interiors 1986. In the Pink: Creeks Boutique, Paris," vol. 174, n° 11, Sept. 1986, pp. 128-133.

Architecture d'Aujourd'hui

Trelcat, Sophie, "Nuits glamour et cantine de luxe" (St. Martins Lane Hotel, Sanderson Hotel, London and Bon restaurant, Paris), n° 330, Sept.-Oct. 2000, pp. 90-97.

Fitoussi, Brigitte, "Philippe Starck, bar restaurant Félix à Hong Kong" Oct. 1995, n° 301, pp. 112-113.

Starck, Philippe, "Salon de coiffure Coppola à Milan," n° 178, Dec. 1991, pp. 146-149.

Fitoussi, Brigitte, “Paramount Hotel, New York,” n° 273, Féb. 1991, pp. 148-151.

Chaslin, François, “Biennale de Venise,” n° 270, Sept. 1990, pp. 10-13.

Fitoussi, Brigitte, “Brasserie Asahi Beer, Tokyo”, *ibid.*, pp. 188-192.

Robert, Jean-Paul, “Le Nani Nani de Starck,” n° 270, *ibid.*, pp. 78-80.

Fitoussi, Brigitte, “Le Royalton à New York,” n° 261, Féb. 1989, pp. 70-74.

Id., “Philippe Starck,” n° 237, Feb. 1985, pp. 85-98.

Architecture Intérieure Créé

“Los Angeles. Une entrée par la grande porte, l'hôtel Mondrian,” n° 278, Sept.-Oct. 1997, pp. 78-83.

“Plein cadre Starck” (Le Baron vert, Osaka), n° 247-248, April-May 1993, pp. 76-81.

Colin, Christine, “Paramount Hotel,” n° 239, Oct.-Nov. 1990, pp. 147-150.

Id., “Teatriz Ole ! Un restaurant à Madrid,” n° 235, March 1990, pp. 114-121.

Fillion, Odile, “Café Costes à Paris,” n° 202, Sept. 1984, pp. 76-81.

Architecture Mouvement Continuité

Tasma-Anargyros, Sophie, “Philippe Starck à Tokyo. Le restaurant Manin : une architecture spectacle,” n° 19, Feb. 1988, pp. 80-81.

Breitman, Marc, “Philippe Starck designer architecte,” n° 7, March 1985, pp. 26-31.

Art and Design

Froment, Jean-Louis, “The Art of Architecture. The French Pavilion Venice,” vol. 6, n° 3-4, 1990, pp. 26-29.

Artnews

Grauman, Brigid, “Philippe Starck, Future Perfect,” vol. 88, n° 6, Summer 1989, pp. 90-92.

Art Press

Trelcat, Sophie, “Philippe Starck, le signe et la fonction,” n° 231, Jan. 1998, pp. 49-53.

Braunstein, Chloé, “Starck se met à table,” special issue n° 7, 1st trimester 1987, pp. 47-49.

BàT, Bon à tirer

Synave, Catherine, “Les verriers en fusion” (Daum glasses), n° 145, Sept. 1992, pp. 22-27.

Blueprint

Roux, Caroline, “It's Showtime” (St. Martins Lane Hotel, London), n° 165, Oct. 1999, pp. 56-61.

Field, Marcus, “Let Them Eat (Organic) Cake...” (Seven Eleven, Japon), n° 154, Oct. 1998, pp. 24-25.

Anderton, Frances, “Cooler Than Thou” (Mondrian Hotel, Los Angeles), n° 137, March 1997, pp. 32-34.

Betsky, Aaron, Flutsy, Steven, “Dream City. Reinventing Los Angeles,” *ibid.*, pp. 22-25.

Rawsthorn, Alice, “The World According to Starck” (including Terence Conran, Alberto Alessi and Tom Dixon interviews to coincide with the exibihition of the Design Museum, London), n° 98, June 1993, pp. 21-27.

Popham, Peter, "Paperweight Architecture" (Nani Nani et La Flamme d'or, Tokyo), n° 68, June 1990, pp. 40-44.

Poynor, Rick, "Armchair Theatre" (Teatriz restaurant, Madrid), ibid., pp. 46-48.

Burt, Jillian, "The Hippest Hotel in Manhattan" (Royalton Hotel, New York), n° 53, Dec. 1988-Jan. 1989, pp. 22-26.

Casabella

Polano, Sergio, "Passati prossimi, futuri anteriori," vol. 60, n° 635, June 1996, pp. 40-45.

Casa Vogue

"Designer Talk. Philippe Starck. Confessions of a Designer," n° 246, Nov. 1992, pp. 112-119.

Premoli, Francesca, "The Sign of Starck" (Royalton Hotel, New York), n° 207, April 1989, pp. 188-193.

City

Palette, Jim, "Philippe Starck," n° 42, May 1988, pp. 102-103.

Boissière, Olivier, "Le design et le mobilier français," n° 16, Oct. 1985, pp. 52-58.

Cnac Magazine

Bidaine, Philippe, "La critique à travers l'émotion," n° 46, July.-Sept. 1988, p. 35.

Connaissance des arts

Jodidio, Philip, Blanc, Dominique, "L'Ensad fait peau neuve," n° 556, Dec. 1998, pp. 62-63.

Id., "Les Costes," n° 521, Oct. 1995, pp. 94-99.

Wolf, Alfred, Jodidio, Philip, "L'âme de Hong-Kong" (interior of the Peninsula Bar, Hong-Kong), n° 516, April 1995, pp. 78-85.

Jodidio, Philip, "Les joyeux compères de Groningue," n° 514, Feb. 1995, pp. 110-119.

Création

"Design" (Daum vases), n° 43, Dec. 1988-Jan. 1989, pp. 56-57.

D'A d'Architectures

Lenfant-Valère, Carine, "Architecture navale. Sur la vague de l'expérimentation" (Bénéteau), n° 85, July-Aug. 1998, pp. 15-26.

Rambert, Francis, "L'architecture du propre" (Vitry-sur-Seine factory), n° 56, June 1995, p. 33.

Daidalos

Klem, Klaus, "Philippe Starck et Andrée Putmann," n° 62, Dec. 1996, pp. 118-129.

Designers' Journal

Redhead, David, "Dream Sequence" (Teatriz restaurant, Madrid), n° 59, July-Aug. 1990, pp. 72-76.

Design Report

Muller, Birgit, "Yuppie-Yoo" (Yoo apartments, London), n° 12, Dec. 2000, p. 16.

Design Week

Manuelli, Sara, "Switched On" (Hudson Hotel, New York), vol. 15, n° 46, Nov. 2000, pp. 27-30.

— Barett Rhodes, Melissa, "Room with Hue" (St Martins Lane Hotel, London), vol. 71, n° 1, Jan. 2000, pp. 123-131.

Rombough, Howard, "XO Set" (interview with Philippe Starck by Gérard Miallet), vol. 8, n° 23, June 1993, pp. 16-17.

Diseño Interior

"Hotel Sanderson en Londres," n° 100, Oct. 2000, pp. 148-156.

Restaurante Bon en Paris," n° 98, July 2000, pp. 156-159, 193.

"Hotel St Martins Lane en Londres," n° 97, june 2000, p. 148-157, 192.

Rodriguez y Arino, Marta, "Philippe Starck," *ibid.*, pp. 94-95

Lorenzo, Soledad M, "Restaurante Félix" (Peninsula Hotel, Hong-Kong), n° 48, 1995, pp. 46-51, 76-77, 82.

Domus

Sudjic Deyan, "Samsonite, ogetti, objects," n° 832, Dec. 2000, pp. 164-165.

Bullivant, Lucy, "St Martins Lane. Il senso della sorpresa," n° 823, Feb. 2000, pp. 48-55.

Hamaide, Chantal, "Buoni prodotti per consumatori buoni. Il progetto visionario di Starck," n° 815, May 1999, pp. 82-89.

"Philippe Starck. Il nuovo Adamo nel terzo millenio con le mani pulite" (Philippe Starck interviewed by François Chaslin in *Interview*), n° 800, Jan. 1998, pp. 84-89.

Capella, Juli, "Mondrian Hotel, Los Angeles," n° 794, June 1997, pp. 57-61.

Picchi, Francesca, "Bar, ristorante e discoteca a Hong Kong: The Peninsula Hotel," n° 774, Sept. 1995, pp. 58-62.

Romanelli, Marco, "Architetture a Tokyo tra il 1987 e il 1990" (Nani Nani and La Flamme d'or, Tokyo), n° 721, Nov. 1990, pp. 46-55.

Elle

Baudot, François, "Les objets ont-ils une âme? Le monde selon Starck," n° 2724, March 16, 1998, pp. 104-113.

Elle Decoración

Baudot, François, "Jungla de cristal, en exclusiva: la casa del diseñador Philippe Starck," n° 38, Oct. 1994.

Elle Décoration

Trétiack, Philippe, "Starck à la folie," n° 106, March 2001.

Baudot, François, "Le volcan Starck prépare son éruption," n° 76, Dec. 1997-Jan. 1998, pp. 56-58.

Pussey, Gérard, "Sur le toit d'une tour mythique de Hong-Kong," n° 55, May 1995.

Dumoulin, Marie-Claire, "Pour Bruno Le Moult-Starck, sa première maison d'architecte," n° 6, Feb.-March 1989, pp. 92-97.

Frame

Preece, Robert, "Headline Hotels " (Paramount, New York, Delano, Miami, Mondrian hotels, Los Angeles), n° 10, Sept.-Oct. 1999, pp. 49-51.

Galeries Magazine

Le Foll, Joséphine, "Architectureà la Biennale de Venise," n° 37, June -July 1990, pp. 70-73.

Graphics International

Morgan, Conway Lloyd, "Good Goods," n° 63, March 1999, pp. 12-13.

Graphis

O'Brian, Heather, "Alessi, une affaire de famille," vol. 53, n° 311, Sept.-Oct. 1997, pp. 40-49, 133-135.

Rothstein, Mervyn, "Chaque jour, le rideau se lève sur les hôtels de Ian Schrager," ibid., pp. 70-76, 141-143.

Russell, Beverly, "Starck, le délirant génie du design," vol. 51, n° 301, Jan.-Feb. 1996, pp. 32-41, 130-132.

I.D. Magazine
Rawsthorn, Alice, "Fire and Ice" (Ian Schrager and Philippe Starck), March-April 1996, pp. 54-57.

Interior Design
Cohen, Edie Lee, "High on Hudson," vol. 72, no 1, Jan. 2001, pp. 190-198.

Barrett Rhodes, Melissa, "Room with Hue" (St Martins Lane Hotel, London), vol. 71, n° 1, Jan. 2000, pp. 123-131.

Cohen, Edie Lee, "L.A. Boogie-Woogie " (Mondrian Hotel, Los Angeles), vol. 68, n° 4, March 1997, pp. 104-111.

Nasatir, Judith, "The Delano," vol. 66, Oct. 1995, p. 92-99.

Cohen, Edie Lee, "Paramount. Ian Schrager Develops. Philippe Starck Designs," n° 61, Dec. 1990, pp. 142-147.

Interiors
Ogundehin, Michelle, "Schrager's Edge " (Sanderson Hotel, London), vol. 159, n° 9, Sept. 2000, pp. 84-88.

Webb, Michael, "Mondrian," vol. 156, n° 3, March 1997, pp. 62-67.

Henderson, Justin, "Royal Flash " (Royalton Hotel, New York), vol. 150, n° 6, Jan. 1991, pp. 114-115.

Truppin, Andrea, "Starck Struck " (La Cigale, Paris), vol. 148, n° 7, Feb. 1989, pp. 121-129, 156.

Id., "Five Uneasy Pieces. Renovation of the Elysee Palace Causes Criticism but Sells New French Furniture," vol. 144, n° 1, Aug. 1984, pp. 140-145, 178, 182.

Interiors for architects and designers
Bevan, Robert, "Starck Staring " (Hudson Hotel, New York), Dec. 2000, pp. 18-20.

Long, Kieran, "Suits Yoo," April-May 2000, pp. 39-40.

Interni
Beaumont, Thierry de, "Starck menu," n° 505, Oct. 2000, pp. 112-117.

Intramuros
Hamaide, Chantal, "Gregg Buchbinder " (Emeco, United States), n° 91, Oct.-Nov. 2000, pp. 54-55, 96-97.

Id., "Du design " (restaurant Bon, Paris), n° 88, April-May 2000, pp. 33-35.

Tasma-Anargyros, Sophie, "Starck peut en cacher un autre," n° 76, April-May 1998, pp. 48-52.

Hamaide, Chantal, "Starck exclusif. Ce que je pense, ce que je crois," n° 71, June-July 1997, pp. II-XI.

Id., "Le Theatron à Mexico, le voyage initiatique," n° 64, April-May 1996, pp. 34-37.

Germain, Christiane, "Architecture, la boutique Hugo Boss, place des Victoires," n° 44, Sept.-Oct. 1992, pp. 32-33.

Anargyros, Sophie, "Philippe Starck joueur, concepteur, technicien, le portrait d'un inventeur," Sept.-Oct. 1987, no 14, pp. 20-27.

Jardin des Modes
Colin, Christine, "La mode et le design," n° 185, Dec. 1994-Jan. 1995, pp. 26-39.

L'Arca
Mandrelli, Doriana O, "Starckmania," n° 70, April 1993, pp. 83-89.

L'Express

Arosio, Enrico, "Philippe Super Starck," n° 3, Jan. 22, 1998, pp. 90-94.

"Les contes d'Hoffmann à l'opéra de Lyon. Décor de Philippe Starck," May 27, 1993, p. 174.

Le Monde

Champenois, Michèle, "Philippe Starck, le populaire est élégant, le rare est vulgaire," Aug. 22, 1998, p. 5.

Le Moniteur Architecture – AMC

"Substances intérieures," Jan. 2001, pp. 57-58.

"Expérience Nîmes," n° 26, Nov. 1991, pp. 35-58.

"Restaurant Teatriz, Madrid," n° 13, July-Aug. 1990, pp. 66-67.

Le Point

Fitoussi, Brigitte, "Philippe Starck... exercices de style," n° 780, 31 Aug. 1987.

Libération

Fevre, Anne-Marie, "Designers de Starck et d'essai," 19-20 Feb. 2000, pp. 38-39.

Fitoussi, Brigitte, "Starck entre en correspondance avec La Redoute," 20 Sept. 1998, pp. 32-33.

"Le Mobilier urbain," Oct. 4, 1994.

Trittoleno, M., "New York: Ian Schrager, hôtelier particulier," Nov. 6, 1990, pp. 37-38.

Sabatier, Patrick, "Signé Starck à Tokyo," 6-7 Jan. 1990, pp. 28-29.

L'Œil

Fitoussi, Brigitte, "La vie en Starck," Sept. 1997, no 488, pp. 32-39.

Madame Figaro

"Philippe Starck, je produis pour exister " (interview by Marc Lambron), n° 17304, 1st April 2000, pp. 26-31.

Maisons Côté Sud

Bittner, Noëlle, "Nuits blanches à Miami " (Delano Hotel, Miami), April-May 1996.

Marie-Claire Maison

Deloffre, Claude, "Le Starck system," special issue, June 2001, pp.11-16.

Modo

Morozzi, Cristina, "Nuova-antica salle d'eau," n° 158, Aug.-Sept. 1994, pp. 25-27.

Novum Gebrauchsgraphik

Neuman, Eckhard, "A Hotel Propectus " (Royalton Hotel, New York), vol. 64, n° 10, Oct. 1993, pp. 26-29.

On Diseño

"Torch for the Winter Olympics at Albertville 92," n° 131, 1992, pp. 112-113.

Serrano Marzo, Manuel, "El teatro Teatriz. Philippe Starck," n° 119, 1991, pp. 106-139.

Ottagono

Dedini, Antonella, Scevola, Annamaria, "The Grand Hotel : Home of Travel " (Paramount Hotel, New York), n° 99, June 1991, pp. 118-147.

Tazzi, Luigi, "Art Versus Architecture " (Biennale de Venise), n° 96, Sept. 1990, pp. 7-18.

Pole Position

Colin, Christine, "La lampe Ray Menta," n° 1, May 1985, pp. 12-13.

The International Design Yearbook

Starck, Philippe, "Manifesto for an Autocracy of Design," 1997, pp. 6-9.

Morgan, Conway Lloyd, "Designer in the High Castle," 1997, pp. 10-13.

The Sunday Telegraph Magazine
"The Immaculate Concept," 11 Jan. 1998, pp. 32-35.

WEBSITES

Alessi	www.alessi.it
Aprilia	www.aprilia.com
Actual	www.actual.at
Alfi	www.alfi.de
Baleri	www.baleri-italia.com
Bénéteau	www.beneteau.fr
Big	www.big.de
Biofa	www.biofa.com
Cassina	www.cassina.it
Daum	www.daum.fr
J.-C. Decaux	www.jcdecaux.com
Dieau	www.dieau.com
Driade	www.driade.com
Duravit	www.duravit.com
Ecover	www.ecover.com
Emeco	www.emeco.net
Eurostar	www.eurostar.com
Fiam	www.fiamitalia.it
Flos	www.flos.net
Fossil	www.fossil.com
FSB	www.fsb.de
Fujifilm	www.fujifilm.com
Groninger Museum	www.groninger-museum.nl
Hansgrohe	www.hansgrohe.com
Heller	www.helleronline.com
Hoesch	www.hoesch.de
Kartell	www.kartell.it
K-Way	www.kway.fr
Kleisdesign	www.kleisdesign.com
Laguiole	www.knives-laguiole.com
L'Oréal	www.loreal.com
Maletti Group	www.malettigroup.com
Mikli	www.mikli.fr
Monnaie de Paris	www.monnaiedeparis.fr
Moulin Roty	www.moulinroty.fr
OAO	dschepens@oao-food.com
Otis	www.otis.com
Rapsel	www.rapsel.it
Rotomod	www.rotomod.com
Samsonite	www.samsonite.com
St Georges	www.eauxstgeorges.fr
Philippe Starck	www.philippe-starck.com
Target	www.target.com
Thomson Multimédia	www.thomson-multimedia.com
La Valoise	www.watercooler.ch
Vitra	www.vitra.com
Virgin	www.virgin.com
Vuitton	www.vuitton.com
Wolford	www.wolford.com
Winia	www.winia.nl
XO	www.XO-Design.com
YOO	www.yooarehere.com

Graphic Design
Jean Yves Cousseau

Printed in France by
imprimerie Corlet, Condé-sur-Noireau,
in February 2003.
N° 70098